The Color Printer Idea Book

D0753798

The Color Printer Idea Book

Kay Hall

NO STARCH PRESS
SAN FRANCISCO

Publisher: William Pollock
Project Editor: Karol Jurado
Production Assistance: Carol Lombardi
Cover Design: Cuttriss & Hambleton
Interior Design: Derek Yee Design
Illustrators: Sally Marts, Derek Yee Design
Compositor: Magnolia Studio
Copyeditors: Carol Lombardi, Beverly McGuire
Distributed to the book trade in the United States and Canada by Publishers Group West, 1700 Fourth Street, Berkeley, CA 94710, phone: 800-788-3123 or 510-548-4393, fax: 510-658-1834.
For information on translations or book distributors outside the United States, please contact No Starch Press directly:

No Starch Press
555 De Haro Street, Suite 250, San Francisco, CA 94107
phone: 415-863-9900; fax: 415-863-9950; info@nostarch.com; http://www.nostarch.com

Library of Congress Cataloging-in-Publication Data
Hall, Kay.
      The color printer idea book : 40 cool and practical things you can make
with your inkjet printer! / Kay Hall.
          p. cm.
      Includes index.
      ISBN 1–886411–20–4 (alk. paper)
      1. Computer art. 2. Handicraft—Data processing. 3. Color Printers
(Data processing system).   I. Title.
TT869.5.H35   1997
745.5—dc21   97-35775

This book is dedicated to my parents, Bill and Estelle Higgins, who have always been dedicated to me.

Table of Contents

CHAPTER 6
MORE TECHNIQUES FOR COMPUTER CRAFTING

PART 2 PROJECTS

PART 3 RESOURCES
APPENDIX A
SELLING WHAT YOU MAKE

Acknowledgments

First let me thank the team at No Starch Press for their willingness to break new ground with this book. Vendor support for this project was overwhelming. Thanks to all of the printer companies who readily supplied printers, ink, and media. A particular thanks goes out to John at Weber-Valentine; Steve, Marilyn, and Sandra at Micro Format; Mike and Michelle at Janlynn; Kevin at Fiskars; Dennis of D. Brooker & Associates; and Patrick at Hanes. All of them fielded my numerous, and sometimes unusual requests, cheerfully and speedily.

The printing enthusiasts I have met on CompuServe, America Online, and especially on the PALs listservs are too numerous to list, but they have been invaluable to me. I often turned to these online friends when I got stuck on a certain project or needed a boost of creativity.

Others who deserve my thanks include Annette, Autumn, Caleb, Cheryl, Ches, Jill, Libby, Mary, Sally, and Vicki who took on various tasks as well as providing much-needed encouragement along the way. My treasured friend LuAnn Sorey spent countless evenings with me cutting, gluing, glittering, and greatly improving the project samples, even though she had her hands full preparing to move to another state. More than that, she made it fun. I miss you, Lu!

Nicole Sorey started out helping take care of my children, but ended up making significant contributions to the book by proofreading, brainstorming projects with me, and giving me another viewpoint as I went along. Thank you, Nicole . . . not bad for someone who had just turned seventeen.

Last but not least, special thanks to my incredible husband, E.W., who, in addition to researching information, entering data, and helping with the index, did a year and a half of Super Dad duty to free me up for writing.

—*Kay Hall*

Preface

It's been at least 25 years since my parents took me to that open house at a college computer lab. I distinctly recall a noisy contraption, about the size of a washing machine, plunking down rows of zeros on the page. As the green striped paper inched out of the printer line by line, a pattern began to emerge. We soon recognized it as the familiar image of Snoopy atop his dog house. Perhaps there really is a good use for computers after all, I remember thinking. That thought was quickly dashed, though, when I was shown next the three rooms that housed the computer needed to generate the simple cartoon dog.

Certainly, a lot has changed since that day when I saw my first "computer craft." Snoopy now flies his doghouse across our home computer screen, taking breaks to teach geography to my children. We have a computer and printer that fit side by side in a briefcase. Best of all, computer-generated cards and gifts are a part of our everyday life.

I'm delighted to have the opportunity to share these creative printing techniques and ideas with you. I hope that you will enjoy them as much as I do.

Before you jump in to the projects outlined in Part II of this book, you'll need to learn some basic information and techniques from both the computing and the crafting disciplines. We'll also introduce you to materials and equipment that will add to your computer crafting enjoyment. You probably already have a lot of what you'll need, but stand by to hear about more ingenious things you'll want to try out!

1

Part 1 **Tools and Techniques**

Computer Hardware for Printing

To do colorful computer crafting, you need a graphics-capable computer and a color printer. Of course, the newer, faster, and swoopier (a technical term coined by Dave Barry) your computer, the better. However, don't let the lack of the latest, greatest processing power discourage you—my fourth grader's class creates delightful crafts with a color printer driven by a Macintosh built the year he was born.

COLOR INKJET PRINTERS

Inkjet is the generic name for the category of printers that includes Apple StyleWriters, Canon Bubble Jets, Hewlett Packard DeskJets and DeskWriters, the Epson Stylus series, and Lexmark JetPrinters and WinWriters. With inkjet technology, liquid ink from a small tank flows to a *print head* punched with tiny holes through which the ink is squirted onto the page with amazing precision.

In contrast, *laser printers,* such as the Hewlett Packard LaserJets, use dry powdered toner that is fused to the page with heat and pressure. In *dot matrix printers,* tiny pins hammer an inked ribbon into the page, leaving the ink behind.

Color inkjets are by far the dominant printer on home desktops, so that's what we'll focus on.

GETTING TO KNOW YOUR INKJET

A little up-front investigation and experimentation with your printer will build your confidence, as well as save you headaches later on. Filling out the worksheet on page 158 will help you become acquainted with your printer's characteristics.

CHARACTERISTICS TO KNOW

Every printer model is different and has certain features and specifications you can't change, but might need to know about for one reason or another. Learning about these characteristics also comes in handy when you're shopping for a new printer.

Cartridges and Inks

In most printers, you replace either the black or a multicolor cartridge, but some cartridge sets allow you to change out each color individually. Your printer's manual will tell you what type of replacement cartridges to get. Record the cartridge part numbers on your worksheet for handy reference.

Most computer crafters use enough ink to develop an avid interest in less expensive third-party ink cartridges and refill kits. Printer manufacturers discourage using these, but many printer owners claim great success refilling cartridges or purchasing clone cartridges. Using these aftermarket

DRY INK PRINTERS

Inkjets are a great way to print beautiful images cheaply, and they're phenomenally popular, but a recently introduced technology is also intriguing to many computer crafters. Dry ink printing, featured in Alps MicroDry printers, uses ribbons instead of ink cartridges. Because the ink doesn't splatter, the dots are very crisp, and the resulting image quality is excellent.

These printers also offer optional opaque white and metallic inks that let you produce a stunning look on any color paper, including black. Better yet, the ink is permanent—waterproof and lightfast. With special media, dry ink printers let you print bumper stickers, waterslide decals, temporary tattoos, and exceptionally durable heat transfers.

Unfortunately, dry ink printers print slowly, and they can't print on envelopes or any textured surface. These factors relegate the current crop to the "specialty" category. Still, a dry ink printer is an excellent second printer for any crafter, especially scrapbooking or transfer enthusiasts.

products may affect your warranty protection in some cases, so read your manual carefully before going this route.

Depending on your printer, you may be able to use specialty ink cartridges, such as those with neon ink, photographic ink, dye sublimation transfer ink, or indelible black ink. Check with the manufacturer of your printer and third-party suppliers to find out what options are available for your particular model.

At this writing, no inkjet printers made for the home user have waterproof or lightfast color ink, although this is sure to change eventually. Black inks have improved dramatically, and an increasing number of printers now ship with permanent black ink.

To see how your printer's ink holds up to water, you might want to do some informal testing, keeping in mind that the drying time allowed after printing and the choice of paper can greatly affect your results. Likewise, to test the effects of light exposure, put some printouts in a window and check them weekly for fading or color shifts.

Paper Path

The term *paper path* refers to the route a page takes as it travels through the printer. As a practical matter, your printer's paper path determines how you should load the paper in the tray. This isn't always trivial, especially when using predesigned paper, when printing on both sides of the sheet. With respect to paper path, inkjet printers fall into three categories: (1) front-, (2) top-, or (3) back-loading. With front-loading printers, the paper makes a 180° turn as it rolls through the printer (that is, it goes in "face down" and comes out "face up"); with back- or top-loading printers, the paper makes no more than a slight bend. Some printers provide an optional straight paper path for heavier papers accessed from a "trap door" in the back. Consult your manual or run some paper-loading tests on your printer to investigate all your options. Fill in the results on the worksheet for future reference.

....

TIP: *Even with diagrams to go by, it's easy to make errors, especially when you're in a hurry. Before you waste expensive paper and lots of effort, slow down and concentrate. For your most critical projects, take the time to run drafts and mockups on plain paper first.*

....

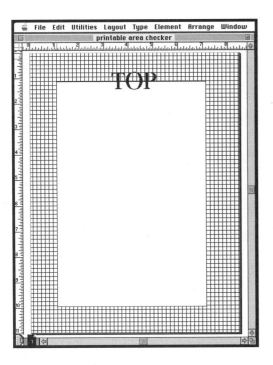

Figure 1-1. Print a test document like this to reveal the printable area of your printer. (White space in the center conserves ink.)

DYES VERSUS PIGMENTS

Inkjet printer inks are either dye-based or pigment-based. To understand the difference, think of dye-based ink as food coloring, and pigment-based ink as house paint. Pigmented inks are waterproof and hold up to light exposure much better, but unfortunately can't provide the range of color we've become accustomed to with dye-based inks.

All current desktop inkjets use dye-based color inks, but some manufacturers (Hewlett Packard and Lexmark at present) have switched to pigmented black inks. In addition to permanence, pigmented blacks are more opaque and photocopy better than their dye-based counterparts. A disadvantage is that these pigmented inkjet inks dry more slowly, but crafters can use that to advantage on powder embossing projects like the White-on-Black Design project on page 88.

Printable Area

Even though your printer will handle paper at least as large as 8 1/2 x 14 inches, it can't, unfortunately, print all the way to the edges on any size paper. The unprintable areas along each side of the page represent the minimum margins you can use in your designs. Your printer's manual should list the margins and total printable area for different paper sizes, or you can test for yourself (see Figure 1-1).

Typically, inkjet printers can print much closer to the top (or leading) edge of a page than to the bottom (or trailing) edge. To center a design on the page, you'll have to compensate for these unequal margins. In some programs, this is as simple as clicking a check box. In others, you'll have to adjust the design yourself. To do this, create a simple test page with an object centered in your computer document and print it out. Fold the page in half

to see if the object is physically centered and, if not, measure and record the offset from center and its direction on your worksheet. Back at the computer, shift the entire contents of your page the same amount as the offset in the opposite direction and test again. In our Stationery project on page 46, Color Plate 2, for instance, the original printout measured 0.2 inches to the right of center, so we moved everything 0.2 inches to the left. Check your software manual to learn how to move things a specific distance in your particular program or just use trial and error.

Speed

Printer speed, measured in pages per minute (ppm), is a loudly touted specification among manufacturers, but it doesn't really reflect how long it takes to print a crafter's typical page. Page-per-minute figures are kind of like a car's maximum miles per hour—top speed on the track is a far cry from how fast you'll be able to go in day-to-day traffic.

Use ppm figures to gauge the relative speed of various printers when you're shopping for a new one, but only as the tiebreaker when deciding between otherwise equal printers.

Maximum Resolution

A printer's resolution, measured in dots per inch (dpi), is considered a major point of comparison, although it is just one of many factors that influence print quality. In fact, the latest software technologies and special photo ink sets are making dpi increasingly irrelevant. Dots per inch can also get confusing, because some printers list different dpi figures for color, black and white, or vertical and horizontal dimensions. You will get the maximum dots per inch only at the printer's highest quality setting and, with some printers, only on special paper. All this suggests that you shouldn't get too hung up on dpi when choosing a printer—let your eye be the judge instead. If possible, print your own sample file on different printers and compare their results side by side. Once you've bought a printer, though, knowing its maximum resolution will be helpful when buying paper or choosing scanner settings, so we've made room on the worksheet for you to record it.

SETTINGS TO UNDERSTAND

The quality and colors you see on a given printed page depend on the ink, the media (paper or other), and the various print settings you select. Change any of these variables and you will get different—sometimes drastically different—results.

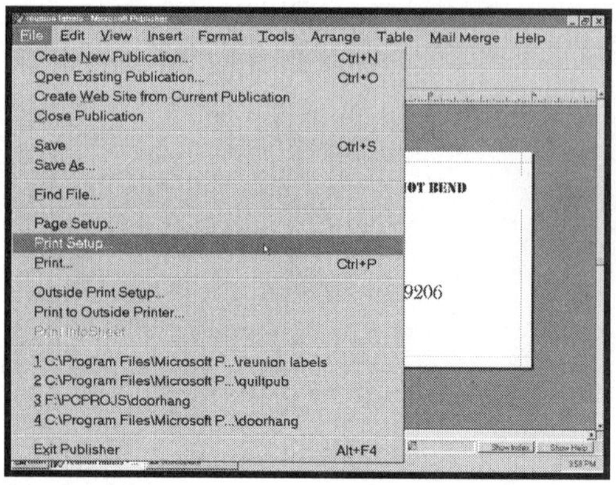

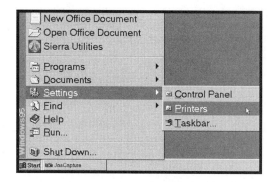

Figure 1-2. Command sequence—first the pull-down menu (above) then the dialog box (right)—for accessing printer properties in Microsoft Publisher.

Figure 1-3. Command sequence—via two pop-up menus—for accessing printer properties (to set defaults) from the Windows 95 Start Button.

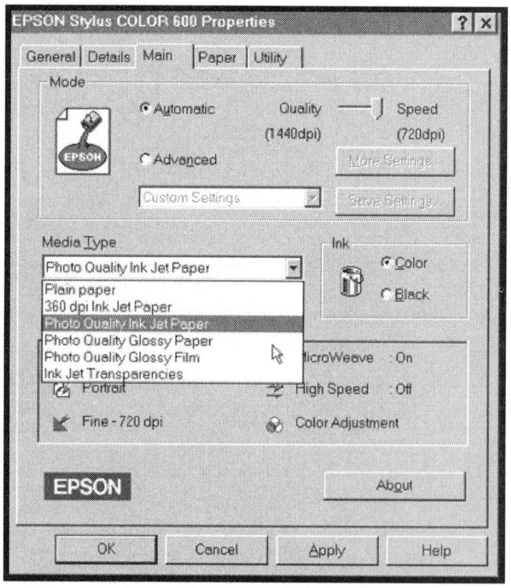

Figure 1-4. Printer properties are specified in Windows 95 with tabbed dialog boxes. This example is from the Epson Stylus 600's Properties box. Clicking the Advanced radio button makes more options available.

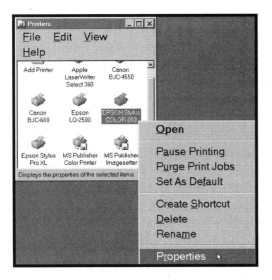

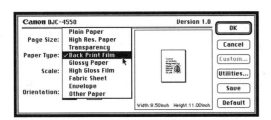

Figure 1-5. On a Macintosh, media type is chosen from a pop-up menu under Page Setup. This example is from a Canon BJC-4550 printer.

WHERE DO I FIND THESE SETTINGS?

ON A PC

The steps for finding printer settings vary from application to application in Windows 3.1 and Windows 95. Once you're in your application, choose Print Setup or Print from the File menu, and look for media, print quality, and other advanced print settings, often reached through the Properties button. Figure 1-2 shows the sequence required to access printer properties in Microsoft Publisher.

In Windows 95, you can also change settings and make them the defaults by pressing the Start button and choosing Settings, then Printers. Right-click the icon for your printer and choose Properties from the pop-up File menu (as shown in Figure 1-3). You'll see various setup options here as shown in Figure 1-4.

Some printers allow you to name and save groups of settings to use again later—a useful feature if you plan to repeat project types with complicated settings. Check your printer's manual to see if you can do this and to learn how.

ON A MACINTOSH

The media settings shown in Figure 1-5 are found under the Page Setup command in the File menu. Print quality settings (shown in Figure 1-6) can be adjusted, and advanced options (such as intensity) reached, under the Print command in the File menu or by pressing command-P (⌘-P).

SOFTWARE-SPECIFIC OPTIONS

Some software, such as Sierra Online's Print Artist (a popular craft program we'll talk about more in Chapter 2), adds its own Print Options or similar command under the File menu. This command presents specialized options, as shown in Figure 1-7, available only when printing from that particular software.

Figure 1-6. A print quality menu appears after you select the Print command on a Macintosh. In this example from a Hewlett Packard DeskWriter 680C, advanced features are accessed by clicking on the Options... button.

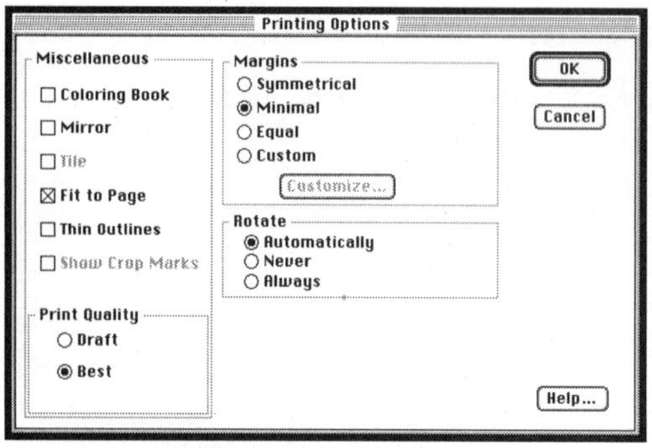

Figure 1-7. Sierra's Print Artist has its own special printing features.

Media Type

Each inkjet model has its own unique settings and procedures for selecting them, but we can make a few generalizations. Your printer's settings should include a choice of media types such as plain paper, coated paper, transparency film, and so on. Among other things, the selection you make tells the printer the amount of each color of ink to put on the page to optimize print quality for a specific paper. Printer manufacturers fine-tune their software to match their own brands of media, but don't be afraid to try different settings with different media to see what looks best to you.

Print Quality

With inkjets, print quality and media settings are tied together. Not all quality settings are available for all media choices and vice versa, so don't be surprised if some settings seem to be missing.

You may find it helpful to fill in the grid of media types and quality settings on the printer worksheet. With most color inkjets, you'll have a choice of three or four settings such as Super, Best, Normal, Draft, and so on. Your quality selection affects both the number of dots placed on the page and the way they are arranged to trick your eye

into seeing a complete spectrum of colors. As a result, a color in a given document can come out quite differently from one quality setting to the next, even when you're printing on the same paper each time.

To limit your printing surprises, create a test document and print it at different settings on each kind of paper you typically use and file the results with your worksheet for reference. Your ideal test document might include black and color text at various sizes, a favorite color photo, black-and-white line art, color clip art, large blocks of color and shades of gray, or other elements, depending on the kinds of images you expect to be printing.

Color Management

The most common complaint about color printers is that the colors on the printed page don't match the colors on the computer screen. Why is that? For one thing, the laws of physics dictate that some onscreen colors simply cannot be reproduced on paper, at least not with an inkjet. And some other colors, such as bright red, are only attained by printing on high-grade, coated paper. Finally, some monitors just don't represent colors very well or may need adjustment.

Figure 1-8. Choosing to print color swatches in Print Artist.

Some monitors, color printers, and operating systems come with color management software that helps you to improve the accuracy of your printed colors. You should explore all the advanced settings your printer software and color management system offers, but still, your results may be disappointing.

If you simply must match a specific color (for a logo, for instance), here's what to do:

1. Create a grid of similarly colored squares on a sample document and print it using the same paper and settings that you plan for your final product.

2. On the printout, find the colored square that matches your target color most closely and use that color, no matter what it looks like on your screen. (Be sure to jot down the color's name or numerical values so you can use that color again when you need it.)

TIP: In Sierra Online's Print Artist (PC version), you can print a sample of every color in the color palette by choosing Swatch from the Print selection list in the Print Preview window. See Figure 1-8.

Getting the colors in photos to turn out right can be especially tricky. Photo editing software, like Adobe's PhotoDeluxe or JASC's Paint Shop Pro, can work minor miracles, but it helps if you use a good photo to start with.

Here's how you can print the best-looking photos possible:

1. Use a high-grade, coated paper and print several copies of a representative section of the photo using different variations (brightness, contrast, etc.) on the same sheet of paper or on a couple of sheets (don't waste this paper—it's expensive!). Be sure to copy down the settings that you use for each sample.

2. Pick the sample that you like best and retrieve its settings.

3. Go back to the original photo and apply those changes to the entire photo. Don't worry about how it looks on your screen—it's what goes on the paper that counts.

Drivers

A *printer driver* is a kind of translation program that allows your application software to speak to your printer and tell it what to do. When you (or someone else) installed your operating system or your printer, one or more drivers were installed, whether you knew it or not. Normally, the printer driver is of no concern to you, but if you have printing problems, it could be because your driver is old. As new versions of applications and operating systems are released, drivers need to be updated to work optimally with the new software. If they're not updated, they sometimes hit snags, which can show up as outright refusal to print or unexpected results on the printed page, even after you've double-checked all your connections and settings.

You can find the latest print drivers (and instructions for installing them) free for the downloading on your printer manufacturer's Web site or BBS, or on commercial online services. Alternatively, call your printer's manufacturer to find out if you have the latest driver and, if not, ask them to mail it to you on a floppy disk—many will send the driver disk to you for free. To see if your system is using the latest driver available, you'll first need to know what driver version you currently have installed.

In Windows 95

To find the version number of the installed driver, click the About button on one of the print setting dialogs as shown in the lower right of Figure 1-4, to get an information screen as shown in Figure 1-9.

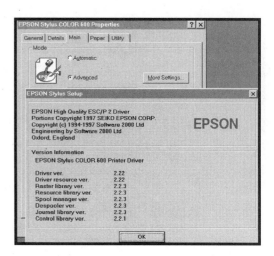

Figure 1-9. Finding information about the printer driver in Windows 95.

On a Macintosh

The driver version number usually appears at the top of the Print and Page Setup dialog boxes, as shown in Figures 1-5 and 1-6.

Software for Crafting

You can begin computer crafting with just a word processor and some clip art, but if you limit yourself to that, you will definitely be doing things the hard way. To enliven your experience, get your design gears turning, and craft the easy way, consider some of the creativity-enhancing software discussed below (contact information for these and other software programs is listed in Appendix C).

CREATIVE PUBLISHING SUITES

The genre of software most closely associated with computer crafts is known in the industry as "creative publishing suites" (see Figures 2-1 and 2-2). Products in this category include Broderbund's Print Shop, Sierra's Print Artist, Corel Print House, Micrografx's Windows Draw Print Studio, and The Learning Company's PrintMaster series. In addition to predesigned layouts for a variety of projects, these packages bulge with *clip art* (computerized images that you can use in your designs), photos, and fonts. They are characterized by an interface that centers around the type of project (sign,

business card, and so on) and an integrated approach that puts all the design components and special effects at your fingertips. Creative publishing suites are a treasure trove of ideas and can't be beat for putting together a nice-looking specialty project quickly.

Though any of these packages will do an admirable job on typical projects such as greeting cards, signs, labels, and business cards, Sierra's Print Artist series goes above and beyond with layouts for hundreds of unusual craft projects, from board games to gift bags (see Figure 2-3). Print Artist's strong craft emphasis, very active user community, wealth of add-on products, and overall strength of its features make it

Figure 2-1. In creative publishing suites, you select the type of project first, as shown here in PrintMaster Gold from The Learning Company.

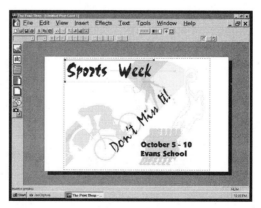

Figure 2-2. Clip art and special effects are easily accessed from the left-hand toolbar in Print Shop Premier Edition.

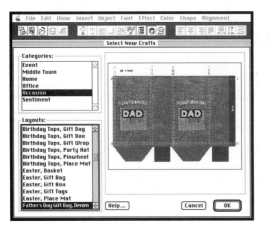

Figure 2-3. Choosing a craft design in Print Artist.

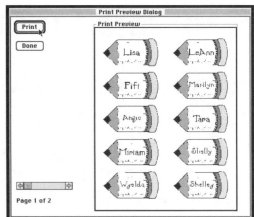

Figure 2-4. The Print Preview screen in Print Artist.

the top choice among avid computer crafters. This category of software is inexpensive enough, though, that many people buy more than one creative publishing program.

....

TIP: *If your application or printer control software offers a Print Preview option (see Figure 2-4), use it to spot printing problems onscreen—before wasting precious time, ink, and paper.*

....

DRAWING SOFTWARE

Regardless of how much clip art you've collected, a time will come when you want to modify some of it or create your own images. This is when a drawing program, such as Corel Draw or Deneba's Canvas, comes in handy.

These programs give you virtually unlimited flexibility to create your own artwork and the ability to do limited page layout as well. You can use them

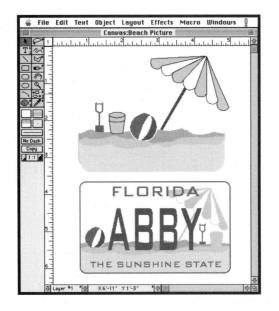

Figure 2-5. Elements from the original clip art image at the top of the screen were rearranged in Deneba's Canvas draw program to suit the design for the license plate at the bottom.

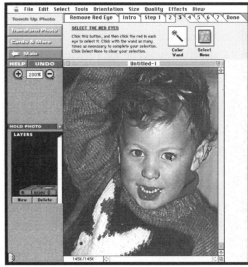

Figure 2-6. The red-eye removal procedure in Adobe PhotoDeluxe.

Figure 2-7. The photo of the baby was combined with the photo of the rose to create the new image.

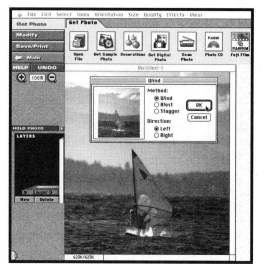

Figure 2-8. Using the Wind filter in Adobe PhotoDeluxe.

to color black-and-white graphics, design your own logo, combine clip art images (as shown in Figure 2-5) to create new images, or draw a treasure map of your back yard.

PHOTO EDITING SOFTWARE

Photo editing, the art of manipulating or enhancing photographs, is one of the most fun and useful things you can do with a computer. Nothing personalizes a craft project more than a photograph. Adobe PhotoDeluxe, oriented toward home users, is one of the most popular photo editing packages. It is inexpensive to buy (or comes bundled with many printers, scanners, and digital cameras) and easy to use, walking you through common tasks like removing redeye (see Figure 2-6), correcting exposure, merging different images, and changing a background.

It's truly amazing what you can do with photo editing software. For instance, I merged a snapshot of my daughter with a stock photo of a rose (see Figure 2-7) to create the image for the Shaped Mouse Pad project on page 116, Color Plate 37.

Not long ago I wouldn't have been able to do this sort of editing without very expensive hardware and software. Now, though, almost any scanner, digital camera, or printer sold comes with these features right in the box. Increasingly, photo editing features are showing up in creative publishing suites and desktop publishing software as well.

Some of the coolest image manipulation magic is done with electronic filters. Applying these to an image, or part of one, produces a variety of effects, such as simulating paint strokes, creating a mosaic, softening focus, feathering edges, or artificially aging a photo (see Figures 2-8 and 2-9). These filters and related painting tools are also responsible for some of the most popular non-photo special effects, such as drop shadows behind images and embossed-look text.

Figure 2-9. Using the Emboss filter in Adobe PhotoDeluxe.

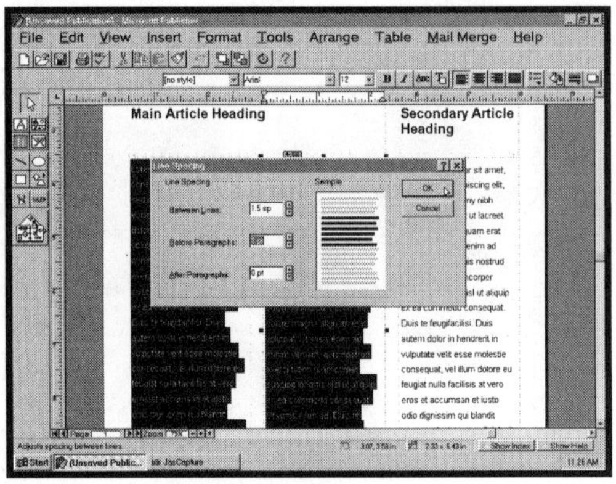

Figure 2-10. Microsoft Publisher features detailed text controls such as line spacing.

Kai's Power Goo from MetaTools is a very unusual subset of photo editing software that you must see to appreciate (but beware, it's addictive!). It lets you bring fun-house effects to faces as you stretch and twist them into wild creations. Any craft project with a "gooed" image is sure to elicit laughter. You can see a sample in the Game Target project on page 60, Color Plate 9.

DESKTOP PUBLISHING SOFTWARE

The capabilities of *desktop publishing* (also called DTP) or page layout software, such as Adobe PageMaker on the high end and Microsoft Publisher (Figure 2-10) on the low end, often overlap with those of creative publishing suites. But, unlike most of the suites, dedicated DTP packages typically allow you to work with multipage documents, place graphics and text precisely, and work with fine typographic controls. These additional features add

to the learning curve of desktop publishing software, but these packages are, nonetheless, the choice for text-heavy documents like newsletters and brochures.

Lately, we've seen project-oriented interfaces added to draw programs, clip art integrated into desktop publishing programs, and more design flexibility added to greeting card programs. As the distinction between various software categories continues to blur, your personal preference really becomes the most important deciding factor.

SPECIALTY SOFTWARE OPTIONS

Although a desktop publishing program or creative publishing suite can handle just about any project, the list of highly specialized software that might be useful in one craft project or another is extensive. These specialty products stand alone or work with your other software. Examples include programs

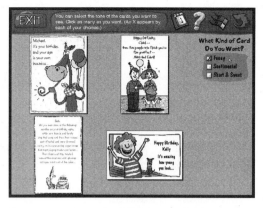

Figure 2-11. CreataCard Plus 2's card selection screen.

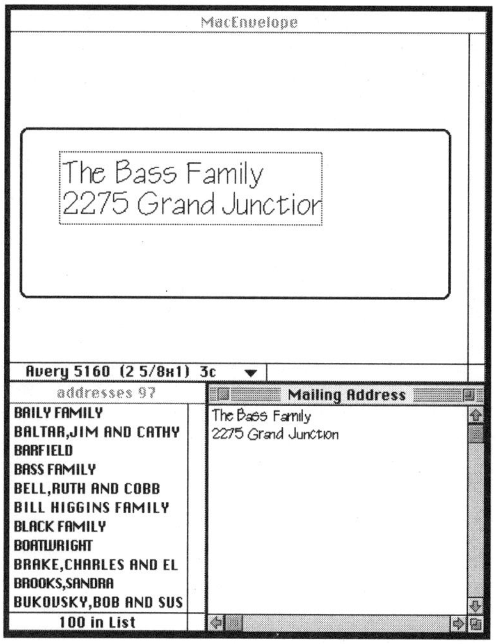

Figure 2-12. Using MacEnvelope to print on Avery 5160 labels.

designed exclusively to generate comic books, stereograms, family trees, children's books, banners, maps, booklets, stickers, badges, buttons, certificates, scrapbook pages, quilt designs, and cross-stitch patterns—in addition to the ones described in the following paragraphs.

Greeting Card Software

Greeting card software has improved so much in the last few years that the results look more like they came from a card shop than from a computer. Alliances with the giants in the greeting card industry are partly responsible for this trend. Search features make it easy to call up the right card for any occasion. Products include American Greetings CreataCard (see Figure 2-11) and Hallmark Connections/Microsoft Greetings. If you bought your printer recently, there's a good chance a greeting card software package came with it.

Label Printing Software

Label software takes care of everything to make label printing painless. Features include the ability to import data from other programs (like databases or word processors) and to begin printing your labels anywhere on the page so that you can finish up partially used sheets. All of the programs support the most popular Avery label formats, and most allow you to create your own layouts as well. The leading products in this category are Avery's LabelPro series, SNX's MacEnvelope (see Figure 2-12), and MySoftware's MyAdvanced LabelMaker.

Calendar Software

Calendars present both layout and calculation challenges. If you want to avoid the hassles, one option is to let a calendar program, like SoftKey's Calendar Creator, take care of the dirty work. It will lay out the grids and fill in the

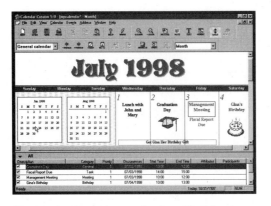

Figure 2-13. Preparing a calendar with Calendar Creator 5.0.

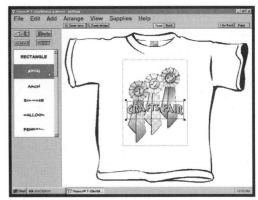

Figure 2-14. Creating a T-shirt design with Hanes T-ShirtMaker & More.

days and dates for you. Calendar programs also let you store lists of birthdays and other family occasions (see Figure 2-13) that will appear on your calendars year after year so that you don't have to type them in each time.

T-Shirt Software

With the incredible popularity of computer T-shirt transfers, it's no surprise that specialty software, such as Hanes T-ShirtMaker & More, has sprung up. Such software is especially handy if you are having trouble reversing designs to mirror image or if you just need design ideas (see Figure 2-14).

Computer Crafting Kits

For those who prefer a more structured approach to computer crafting, several companies make comprehensive kits. Even if you're not interested in a kit, keep an eye out, because these kit companies also sell separate refill supplies you can use in your own projects. (All companies' addresses and other information are listed in Appendix C.)

Kids will enjoy using the PrintPaks multimedia craft kits—from their earliest projects on through their pre-teen computer crafting (see Figure 2-15). This fun-to-use software on CD-ROM

Figure 2-15. The kid-friendly interface of PrintPaks Super Jewelry Kit software.

gives step-by-step instructions for craft activities such as making books, T-shirts, magnets, or jigsaw puzzles. All the necessary supplies are in the box, too. With this package approach, there's ample room for creativity, but little room for error. PrintPaks kits are widely distributed: You can find them in computer and office superstores as well as in mass merchandisers, craft stores, and toy stores.

With both software and print media, Avery's inexpensive Printertainment kits let kids make their own stickers, greeting cards, and more. These products can be found in computer and office superstores and mass merchandisers.

Janlynn Cre8 offers a line of kits for adults that includes both software and supplies. Each kit creates projects, such as memory quilts, pillow toppers, Christmas ornaments, and jewelry, that center around your favorite photos. Cre8's ComputerCrafts kits are sold in many craft stores and camera store chains.

WHERE TO BUY SOFTWARE

If you're lucky enough to have a computer or office superstore nearby, you should find many of the products mentioned above on the shelf. If not, or if you are a Mac user, your best bet is a software catalog like *PC/Mac Connection* or *PC/Mac Warehouse*. Contact information for these retailers, as well as the software publishers (who will often sell direct) is included in Appendix C.

Design Elements

A page's *layout* refers to where the text and graphics are placed on the page and where any cuts and folds will be made. To that underlying matrix, various elements such as the words (also called the *copy* or *sentiment*), typestyles, illustrations, borders, and backgrounds are added.

An understanding of fundamental design principles will serve you well, especially as you veer away from predesigned templates. But for that I'll defer to design gurus like Robin Williams, Roger C. Parker, and Chuck Green, whose excellent books are listed in Appendix D.

LAYOUT TEMPLATES

Just about every kind of software comes with *templates*—ready-made layouts for producing common documents like letterhead, labels, or greeting cards. Templates keep you from having to start with a blank screen, saving significant time and patience in the process. Many applications present template choices automatically when you create a new document, some with "wizards" that step you through the process. Some templates have text and graphics already in place (see Figure 3-1); others use placeholders or guidelines to show you where to put elements you select (see Figure 3-2). Along with precise placement of elements on the page, a template may also specify details such as alignment, rotation, and type attributes.

Any document you or someone else has already completed can function as a template. To use a document as a

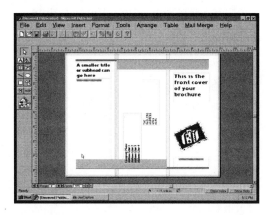

Figure 3-1. This brochure template was accessed through the Wizards feature in Microsoft Publisher 97.

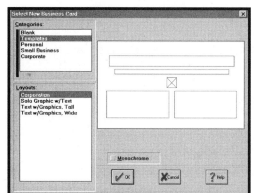

Figure 3-2. From the new document window in Print Artist, you may choose to start with a blank document, a template, or a ready-made document from one of several categories.

How to Make Your Own Template
from Scratch

At some point, you will want to do a project for which you have no template. If you want to print on a specific preprinted brochure paper, for example, you can make your own template. To do so, measure the size and position of the graphic elements on the preprinted paper to help you properly place your own text and graphics on screen. (Or scan a sheet of the paper first at low resolution and insert the image on the bottom layer of your document to use as a guide. Be sure to remove or hide the scanned image before printing.)

When designing your template, take advantage of onscreen rulers and non-printing guidelines if your software offers these features. Depending on the complexity of the preprinted design and your additions, you may be in for quite a bit of trial and error.

Once you've finished your template, print it out on plain paper (preprinted paper can be expensive). Place this test run on top of the real preprinted page and hold the stacked sheets in front of a window or other bright light to see whether elements line up correctly. Make adjustments to your template and repeat the process as necessary. When you are fairly confident of the fit, print directly on the preprinted paper to be sure everything is just right before finalizing your template. Don't forget to save the completed template in a safe place for future use. In addition, if your software supports non-printing notes (text that shows up on your screen but not on the printed page), add a note to your template to record any special instructions for using it.

Some programs save templates in a special file format and in unique folders or directories so that they are easily accessible but protected from accidental modification. See your software's documentation for instructions on saving a document as a template.

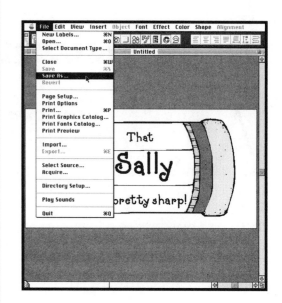

Figure 3-3. Finding the Save As... command in Print Artist.

template, open it in your application, use the Save As command (as shown in Figure 3-3) to create a copy of it with a different name, and then make changes to the copy as desired. By renaming this new document again before saving it, you preserve the original to use again later.

If you find ready-made templates useful, you might want to consider shopping for more of them. Some companies, like Paper Direct and Specialty Publications, offer add-on templates compatible with popular software applications. The online world is another excellent source for templates and sample files. Software publishers sometimes post bonus templates at their Web sites, and many people freely share their own template designs online through e-mail and by posting them in online file libraries.

Fonts

A set of letters, numbers, and symbols of a particular design is called a *font*. (Though subtly different, the terms *typestyle* and *typeface* can be used interchangeably with the word *font* when speaking of desktop publishing.) The style of font you choose will powerfully affect the tone of your project, as you'll notice as you look through our sample projects.

Fonts are very easy to use in your designs—just select a phrase and click an option to change the font. Don't get carried away, though. As a rule, use no more than two or three different fonts on a page unless you're after the "ransom note" look.

Type can generally be classified as either text or display. *Text fonts* are used for setting large blocks of text; they are chosen for their readability, like the font used for this paragraph. *Display fonts* are used for titles, headlines, special effects, and other short stretches of large type, as in the heading for this section or the type used for this chapter's title. *Novelty fonts* are a subcategory of display fonts and include lettering reminiscent of the Wild West, hippie culture, medieval calligraphy, or vintage typewriters. Alphabets made from logs, tools, stitches, or dripping paint are other examples of novelty fonts, which are a lot of fun to work with and make clever additions to your crafts. For example, a snow-capped font is used in the White-on-Black Design project on page 88, Color Plate 23.

TrueType is the preferred font format for inkjet printing and the standard among Windows users. The TrueType fonts that come with one program can generally be used with all other programs that support TrueType.

Most creative publishing suites include hundreds of fonts, and you can obtain additional fonts from companies like Broderbund and Inspire Graphics listed in Appendix C. *Freeware* (no charge) and *shareware* (try before you buy) fonts are plentiful on the Internet and online services.

Clip Art

Just because you can't draw doesn't mean you can't create great-looking projects. Clip art that you can use in your creations is widely available in collections sold online and in computer stores. Because of increased competition, prices and image quality are better than ever.

Like font choice, the clip art you pick can make or break your design. Both the style and content of the art you use will contribute to the effectiveness of your project. In fact, I sometimes select a central piece of clip art first and then design my entire project around it.

Electronic clip art falls into two basic categories, *vector* and *raster*. Vector graphics contain mathematical equations (vectors) that the computer uses to create the graphic on your screen and on the printed paper. Because they're the product of a formula, vector files are compact and scale or stretch nicely when you resize them. Popular vector formats include WMF, CGM, and EPS, but EPS files don't work well with most inkjet printers.

Raster graphics are described by the location and color value of tiny dots, called *pixels*, that make up the image. Raster format images are good to use for very detailed images and photographs, but they don't enlarge very well. Raster graphic files are also larger than vector files, which means they take up more hard disk space and are slower to display on your screen and print. Common raster formats are BMP, GIF, JPG, PCX, and TIF.

Creative publishing suites ship with thousands of pieces of clip art, but some supply the images in a proprietary format—you can't use them easily, if at all, in other programs. GFX files from Print Artist are an example of a proprietary format. On the other hand, the clip art collections you buy separately come in standard formats that you can use with any program. Monster collections, such as those in Broderbund's ClickArt line, come with hundreds of thousands of images on multiple CD-ROMs. As with fonts, you'll find a wealth of shareware and freeware clip art collections online, though much of it is better suited for onscreen display than for printed work.

Subscription services, such as Art Today, are another source of clip art, providing a steady stream of art, or art on demand, for a fee. Whatever you choose, be sure that the format of the clip art you buy is compatible with the software and printer you plan to use.

SCANNING

What if the image you want to use—like an original sketch or a photograph—is on good old-fashioned paper, and not in your computer? Then it has to be *digitized* before you can use it in your computer-generated projects. When you digitize something, you translate it into an electronic form that the computer can understand. When the original art or photograph is on paper, a flatbed *scanner* is the crafter's digitizing tool of choice.

These scanners, which resemble the top portion of a photocopier, are versatile, offer excellent image quality, and are now reasonably priced for the home user. When using a flatbed scanner, you place your image on the scanner's glass, close the cover, launch the scanner's software, and follow a few steps to start scanning.

When shopping for a scanner, compare features like the maximum optical (not interpolated) resolution in dots (the higher the number, the better); the size of the scan area (which should be at least the size of any object you're likely to want to scan—most flatbeds will scan at least a legal-size sheet of paper); and the quality and type of bundled software (scanning software will be included, but how about photo-editing software? Any other software that you might find useful?).

Scanning Services

If you don't have access to a scanner, you can have your images digitized for a small fee at local quick-print shops, office services, or computer service bureaus for this. Most will scan your images and charge you by the piece, but some will rent you time on a scanning station so you can do so yourself. Be sure you get file formats compatible with your home system.

WHAT ARE YOU SCANNING?

The settings you choose for scanning your images will depend on what it is that you're scanning and the final print size and quality you need. Line art (images made up only of solid black lines with no shading), must be scanned differently from paintings, photos, slides, or crayon drawings that your child brings home from school.

Scanning Line Art

When scanning line art, use the same resolution (in dpi) you will use to print it, assuming the image will not be resized. For example, if you'll be printing it at 360 dpi, scan it at 360 dpi. If you plan to resize the scan, calculate the scanning resolution so that you achieve at least the printer's dpi at the new size. For example, if you want to double the size of the resulting image from 2 x 2 inches to 4 x 4 inches, scan the original at twice the printer's resolution. If you plan to shrink it down to half its size, you can scan it in at half the printer's resolution.

Alternatives for Digitizing Line Art

In a pinch, you can digitize line art without a scanner. For instance, if you have a modem that can receive faxes, fax the image to yourself from a public fax machine and use your fax software to receive it. Once you've received the fax, save it in a standard graphic file format (you should find an option to save or export it under the File pull-down menu).

Currently the highest resolution a fax can send is 200 dpi, but if you enlarge the image before you fax it (on a photocopier, for instance) and then fax the enlarged image, you can achieve a higher resolution by squeezing down the faxed image to the original size. If you shrink a 200 dpi fax down to one-half its size, you'll actually end up with a 400 dpi image. Neat trick, isn't it?

For simple graphics, a very low-tech method is to trace by hand or photocopy the image onto clear Mylar or transparency film, then tape the film right onto your screen and "trace" the image with your mouse in a paint or draw program. Once again, enlarging the original improves the results of this method, because imperfections are minimized when the image is reduced.

Scanning Photos

Most flatbed scanners work great for photos. Additionally, there are small sheetfed scanners made specifically for scanning snapshots.

The rule of thumb, if you plan to print from an inkjet, is to scan photographs and most other color images at no higher than one-third of the printer's resolution (assuming no resizing) up to a maximum of about 300 dpi. That is, if you plan to print the image at 720 dpi, scan the photo at 240 dpi or less. If you plan to resize the photo for printing, calculate the scanning resolution so that you achieve the target dpi at the new size as we discussed for line art. Most scanner software will help you with these calculations.

Believe it or not, scanning at a higher resolution than the above rule of thumb suggests will produce huge files, but not necessarily better results. Print some photos saved at various resolutions to find the file size versus dpi tradeoff that works best for you.

Alternatives for Digitizing Photos

In addition to scanning your own photos or using one of the scanning services mentioned above, you have other options for getting photos into digital form:

Photo CD Kodak Digital Sciences offers a very interesting and cost-effective way to digitize photos or slides. You may have encountered this technology, called Photo CD, when you took a roll of standard 35-mm film in for processing and were offered the option to have the pictures returned to you on a CD-ROM. Each Photo CD image is delivered with a range of resolutions, which gives you a lot of versatility. The service also includes a thumbnail hardcopy printout of all the photos placed on each disk. You can even take existing negatives and have them put onto a Photo CD. Your film processor should give you the details you need to use Photo CD files in your projects.

A Note About Copyrights

Just because you can get an image into your computer doesn't mean that you own it. Unless you created the original artwork yourself (or know it is in the public domain), you must obtain permission to use it. For commercial clip art, this permission comes in the form of a license agreement. If you plan to sell the crafts you make, read the license agreement carefully, because some clip art companies won't let you sell your work with their clip art on it unless you pay them additional fees. Restrictions on the use of licensed characters (Disney, Looney Tunes, and so on) and college and professional sports team mascots and logos are very strict. You usually cannot sell or distribute any of these without a costly licensing arrangement, even if you draw them yourself.

When in doubt, don't!

Photos on Floppy Disk Increasingly, storefront and mail-order photo processors offer to put your photos directly onto computer floppy disks for a few dollars. Some will even post your digitized photos to the Internet, so you can download them with a password. The software needed to work with these images is usually included free with the processing. One popular mail-order photo developer that offers this service is Seattle FilmWorks. This is a quick, cheap solution to digitizing photos for use in your projects.

Digital Cameras Digital cameras such as the Kodak DC, Canon Powershot, Casio QV, Sony Mavica, and the Apple QuickTake series (available in most computer or electronics stores) are surging in popularity as prices drop and features improve. Instead of converting a photo on film to digital data, digital cameras record the image electronically from the start, so you skip film and developing altogether.

Video Capture Many of today's multimedia computers come with built-in video features so that you can capture still images from camcorders, video players, or television sets and access them on your computer. Video "grabbers," such as the Snappy from Play (available in computer stores and catalogs), add this capability to an existing system.

Chapter 4

Printable Materials for Inkjets

Y ou can't feed just anything into your inkjet and expect to print on it successfully. To be inkjet-compatible, a sheet of paper must first be thin enough and flexible enough to feed properly and avoid contact with the delicate print mechanism inside. But how can you tell whether the paper you want to use is suitable?

Paper comes in bond, text (or book), and cover weights. Bond is thinner and more flexible than text, which is thinner and more flexible than cover weight. Standard copy paper is bond weight; the paper in this book is text weight; the cover of this book is cover weight. Within each category, you can gauge the relative thickness of a paper using its "basis weight," listed on the package in pounds.

Bond-weight papers (standard copy paper, for example) are fine for printing drafts of your projects and for everyday use, but they aren't substantial enough for most craft projects. *Text-weight* paper, though only a little thicker than bond, has a much more substantial feel to it and holds up better for crafts. The extra thickness also makes the paper more opaque, which can be important for many projects—especially when you're printing on both sides.

Cover-weight paper is thicker and stiffer than either text or bond paper and is generally used for greeting cards, book covers, and the like. Most inkjet printers handle cover-weight paper, or card stock, very well, but check your printer's manual to be sure you won't void your warranty by trying it.

CAUTION: Some high-end inkjets and multifunction machines use a heater to dry the ink faster. If you're using such a printer (the heater will be listed among the product features/specifications in your manual), use only heat-resistant papers like those recommended for laser printers.

Just because something can run through your printer safely doesn't mean that you can print on it with good results. If the surface is too slick, ink will just bead up on it and never dry. If it's too absorbent, the ink will spread, resulting in fuzzy images. (Of course, as resourceful crafters, we'll exploit both of these tendencies.)

TIP: The surface of some specialty stocks is so smooth that the printer's rollers have difficulty grabbing it, resulting in poor feeding. To solve this problem, apply a strip of removable correction tape (try any office supply store) to the leading edge of the sheet on the side of the paper that faces up (where the rollers grab it). Cleaning the rollers with a specially coated cleaning sheet (available at some office supply superstores) may also help.

"Inkjet" Paper

Paper made for inkjets has a specially prepared surface and generally falls into three main categories: plain, coated, and photo grades. *Plain* or uncoated inkjet paper is made with additives to improve whiteness and surface smoothness. It is relatively inexpensive and will give you better results than standard-issue copy paper.

Coated inkjet paper is designed to minimize ink penetration, *dot spread* (your drop of ink bleeding into the paper and thus reducing the sharpness of its edge), and drying times. It's more expensive than plain inkjet paper, but it delivers brighter colors and crisper text and graphics that make it well worth the price.

Photo grade papers are the most expensive (as much as $1.00 per page) and feature glossy coatings optimized for printing photographs. Keep some on hand for special occasions, because the results are absolutely stunning.

TIP: Unless otherwise specified, inkjet paper is coated on only one side. Pay attention to the packaging so you know which side to print on (it's usually the whitest side). Some companies make inkjet paper that is coated on both sides, which is nice for brochures and calendars, among other things.

Colored and Textured Paper

Because inkjet ink is transparent, the color of the underlying paper shows through. So if you print with red ink on green paper, you won't get red (though you might get frustrated!). That's why most inkjet paper is white, and the whiter the better. You may be able to print satisfactorily in color on non-white paper, but stay away from photographs or other designs where color is critical. You can successfully print with black ink on any light- to medium-color paper.

Coated inkjet paper typically has a smooth, *matte* (flat, non-glossy) finish, which offers the best print quality, but inkjets can print nicely on paper with a variety of finishes and textures. Even highly textured surfaces, such as water-color paper or simulated canvas, can be inkjet printed with excellent results.

The finish or texture of your paper can affect the overall look of your project immensely. If you were to print the same design on glossy white stock and on an earth-tone recycled paper, the results would be very different. The glossy white stock will give you a clean, high-tech look; the earth-tone recycled stock will soften your colors and project a certain warmth.

When printing with an inkjet, take advantage of the wide array of papers made for offset or laser printing. Exotic card stocks traditionally used on printing presses, such as Champion KromeKote, Neenah Linen, and Beckett Enhance, are especially coveted for inkjet crafting. You can get your hands on these at paper stores (see Paper Plus and Xpedx in Appendix C) or by cajoling your local printer into selling you a supply. Bring home a few test sheets first, because results vary widely from printer to printer.

CAUTION: Most inkjet printers can print on everything from tracing paper to lunch bags without a problem, but please use common sense to avoid damaging your printer. For instance, you don't want to use anything that will leave a residue or debris.

PREDESIGNED PAPER

A mind-boggling array of decorator paper is available today. The "boutique" paper catalogs, such as Paper Direct, Idea Art, and Queblo, list hundreds of designs, with dozens of coordinating sets and more specialty items than you can imagine. Primarily marketed for laser printers, most of these papers work nicely with inkjets, too.

There are looks to suit just about every taste and occasion—from contemporary patterns to architectural and natural backgrounds, from artsy to strictly conservative graphics. Many papers carry a specific theme, centering around a holiday, a sport, or a concept like excellence, for instance. You can also find a variety of playful, kid-friendly designs.

Both plain and preprinted papers come in dozens of formats, with sizes, shapes, layouts, scores, and perforations to fit many common (and not-so-common) applications. Common formats include corporate identity pieces such as letterhead, envelopes, business cards, and brochures. Note cards, postcards, and labels round out the selection of correspondence tools. Jumbo postcards can double as booklet covers, and matching labels can tie anything from Mason jars to mailing tubes together with a coordinated look. Bolder than their letterhead counterparts, border papers work well for flyers, signs, and certificates.

You can also get paper or card stock that is predesigned (printed, perforated, and/or scored as appropriate) to yield a very specific end-product. Examples are gift boxes, greeting cards, doorknob hangers, cassette or CD inserts, tickets, paper airplanes, table tents, visors, and jigsaw puzzles. (See the list of resources in Appendix B for ideas on where to find specialty papers.)

One disadvantage of catalog shopping is that it's difficult to gauge the look and feel of a particular paper. To solve this problem, most catalogs offer sample kits for a nominal fee, or free samples. If you only need a common format like letterhead, business cards, or brochures, look for preprinted paper in retail outlets such as art supply stores, office superstores, quick-print shops, and even your local Wal-Mart.

EXOTIC PAPERS

Always look for unusual papers to add pizzazz to your creations. Inkjet-compatible metallic paper, for instance, is available in gold and silver and yields surprisingly vibrant colors when printed. See the Metallic-Look Plaque project on page 74, Color Plate 16 for an example. Translucent vellum or tracing paper create an unexpected and very professional look. Or how about using a heat-sensitive paper that changes color when you touch it? We feature this in our Color Change Hidden Message project on page 58, Color Plate 8.

One of the most unique papers I've run across is Virtual Reality Paper from Micro Format, which, when viewed with 3-D glasses, creates the illusion that the printed image hovers over the page. Kids (and young-at-heart grownups) love this stuff.

For paper that makes its own unique statement, try the kinds made from old blue jeans, seaweed, golf course clippings, or recycled money. And for heralding your own statements, 3M Post-It Notes are now available in inkjet-compatible format, including full-page Post-It Signs. (See Appendix B.)

The scrapbook craze has sparked interest in archival (preservation-quality) materials and created demand for *archival paper* for inkjets. Keep in mind, though, that most inkjet ink isn't waterproof or lightfast.

ALL ABOUT ENVELOPES

Finding the right envelope to cradle your computer creation isn't always a trivial matter. Here are some tips, tricks, and basics about a part of the project that most people take for granted.

- For *quarter-fold* cards (an 8 1/2 x 11-inch sheet folded twice, so each card measures 4 1/4 x 5 1/2 inches), use 4 3/8 x 5 3/4-inch envelopes—these may be called announcement size, invitation size, or A2 size. You can buy these at office supply or computer stores or make your own as shown on page 54.

- For *half-fold* cards (an 8 1/2 x 11-inch sheet folded once, so the card measures 8 1/2 x 5 1/2 inches), you can buy 6 x 9-inch envelopes in either *booklet* style (with the opening on the long side) or *catalog* style (with the opening on the short end). White envelopes of either style can be found in office supply stores, paper stores, and some Wal-Marts. Colors are harder to find, but Viking Office Products (listed in Appendix C) is one mail order source for 6 x 9-inch envelopes in bright colors.

- 8 3/4 x 5 3/4-inch envelopes sold in desktop publishing paper catalogs are a better fit for half-fold cards, but they cost up to three times as much as 6 x 9-inch envelopes off the shelf. Keep an eye out, because at least one company is developing

true half-fold size inkjet envelopes for the mass market.

- Printing on store-bought envelopes is notoriously tricky, so be sure to check your printer manual for tips. If you are still having trouble, a sure-fire alternative is to address and/or decorate the envelopes with inkjet-printed labels.

- For odd-sized projects, or when you want an extra-special presentation, you can make envelopes of any size (no computer involved) from magazine pages, gift wrap, wallpaper scraps, and the like. (*The Envelope Mill,* listed in Appendix D, is a lovely book devoted to just this topic.)

- If you'll be mailing homemade envelopes (as opposed to hand delivering them) be sure to take postal regulations into account. You can find out the minimum and maximum dimensions allowed at your local post office or the Postal Service Web site (*http://www.usps.gov*).

- See-through envelopes made of clear cellophane or translucent vellum are always popular with card crafters. Some people print the address on the back of their card or on a separate insert so that it shows through the front of the envelope; others stick an address label on the outside of the envelope itself. Look for cellophane and translucent vellum envelopes at rubber stamp stores or order clear envelopes from Expressive Impressions; translucent vellum ones from LeDesktop (both vendors are listed in Appendix C).

- For a secure bond on cellophane, vellum, or wallpaper envelopes, use pressure-sensitive postage stamps instead of the lick-and-stick kind.

- Protect inkjet-printed envelopes or address labels with a coat of protective spray to help keep the ink from running in case the envelope gets wet in the mail or enclose the addressed card envelope within a larger, clear envelope to protect the whole ensemble in the mail—but still allow your artwork to show through!

- To get a selection of colorful envelopes for free, visit a card shop right after a holiday and ask if you can have the leftovers. Likewise, out-of-date wallpaper books are often free for the asking wherever wallpaper is sold, and the samples are great for decorating cards or making envelopes.

LABELS

When you think of labels, don't stop at the common white address label. Today's inkjet-compatible labels come in many sizes, shapes, designs, and adhesive types. Clear inkjet labels work well, too, and you'll find lots of ways to use them.

TIP: *With the exception of clear, fluorescent, and metallic-finish labels, most laser labels will work fine in an inkjet.*

In the more common label sizes, you have a choice of adhesive types, including permanent, repositionable (meaning you have a second chance to get it in the right place before it bonds for good), and removable or "restickable"(like 3M's Post-It adhesive). Choose among them based on how you plan to use the label. For instance, use permanent or repositionable labels on a jelly jar label, but removable labels when making stickers for younger kids—as we do in our Kids' Stickers project on page 52, Color Plate 5. Nametag stock is also made with a special clothing-friendly adhesive.

Full-sheet (8 1/2 x 11 inches), uncut labels are one of the most useful items a computer crafter can have, because they can be printed and cut to any size or shape. Of course they are great for large applications, like displays and signs, but you can also use them instead of buying full boxes of different, smaller label sizes (custom cut the size you need), or for odd-sized pieces like those in our Photo Standup Paper Doll project (page 112, Color Plate 35). If you don't need many labels, look for ten-sheet packs of full-sheet, uncut labels in the school and office supply department at mass merchandisers. To save money on larger quantities, avoid name brands and consider mail-order sources like Quill and True Basic, both listed in Appendix C.

FILM-BASED MEDIA

Paper isn't the only thing you can print on, of course, and various printable plastic films can be the basis for many fascinating projects. For instance, *opaque* or *photo films*, white plastic sheets in gloss and satin finishes, are formulated to mimic the look of traditional photographs. The clear *transparency film* used to produce overheads for business presentations (visit any office supply store) is also great for many craft applications, such as putting picture windows in cards or making simulated stained glass. We did both in our Imitation Stained Glass angel card project shown on the cover (page 110, Color Plate 34).

MEDIA IN KITS

In Chapter 2, we mentioned some comprehensive kits that include software, media, and other materials. Other kits are available with just media, materials, and instructions for you to use with your own software. Among these are Rayven's Mouse Pad Kit, D. Brooker and Associates' Holo-Graf-Craft Kit, and Avery's various nametag and badge kits. See Appendix C for contact information.

Appliqué film is adhesive-backed polyester that comes in glossy- or matte-finish transparent sheets, as well as in opaque white. It is virtually weatherproof and, like full-sheet paper labels, quite versatile. *Inkjet vinyl* is similar, but is thinner and stretches so that it conforms better to irregular surfaces.

Back print film, so named because you print in reverse on the back side of these translucent sheets, is designed for applications where printouts are mounted on top of a diffuse light source, such as at trade show booths. The vividness of images displayed in this way makes them very high impact.

As the name suggests, *window cling film*, available in white and clear, readily sticks to glass and other smooth surfaces using static cling. It is wonderful for portable or temporary use, because it leaves no residue on the underlying surface and can be reapplied several times. We use this in our Game Target project on page 60, Color Plate 9.

Another of my favorite printable materials is inkjet-compatible *shrink plastic*. These thin plastic sheets shrink (in an oven) and thicken to create hard plastic items bearing the printed images at less than half their original size. The Antique Photo Pin on our cover (page 108, Color Plate 33) is made with shrink plastic.

TIP: *Most film-based media are very slow to dry, so be sure to allow extra time when using them. Also remember to handle the freshly printed pages carefully to avoid smearing.*

FABRIC

Most people are surprised, as I was, to learn just how easy it is to print on fabric with an inkjet printer. Simply iron freezer paper (from the grocery store) onto the back of a piece of pre-washed 100% cotton fabric (such as muslin or percale) and cut to size. Now you can feed it through your printer just like any other paper.

Fabric carrier from Micro Format is an alternative to freezer paper. Instead of heat activation, it uses a pressure-sensitive adhesive. Fabric carrier is easier to use than freezer paper in some ways, but it's much more expensive.

If you're hesitant about these roll-your-own approaches, you can get ready-to-print fabric sheets from a number of commercial sources. One such source is the refill kit for Mattel's Barbie Fashion Designer CD-ROM. In addition to cotton, it also includes tricot fabric sheets (recommended only for printing solid colors because adjacent colors will bleed together on all synthetics).

Canon markets percale fabric sheets for its printers and includes fixative packets, which add a level of washability. Iron-on fabric sheets are available in Janlynn Cre8's ComputerCrafts line, and June Tailor makes printer-ready fabric in pastel colors.

For two very different looks, try inkjet coated artists' canvas (like the material artists use for traditional oil paintings) and satin-finish polyester sheets. Examples of fabric printing projects include the Faux Embroidery (page 78, Color Plate 18), the No-Sew

Pillow (page 80, Color Plate 19), and the Shaped Mouse Pad (page 116, Color Plate 37).

CAUTION: *Unfortunately, most inkjet-printed fabric is not washable—rinsing it, even in plain water, will cause the ink to run. To avoid disappointment, plan projects that won't need to be washed or otherwise exposed to excessive moisture; or use transfer paper, as discussed below.*

Heat Transfer Paper

Transfer paper, as the name implies, lets you transfer an image from something that is inkjet-printable to something that is not. You load this specially coated paper into the inkjet printer and print your design onto it. Place the paper onto the T-shirt (or whatever) and press both with an iron. The heat and pressure of the iron melts the paper's film layer enough to encapsulate the ink and bond to the fabric. You then peel away the paper's backing to reveal a vivid, permanent image on your T-shirt like the one shown on page 56, Color Plate 7. Read the manufacturer's instructions carefully for details on the transfer process.

NOTE: *Because both inkjet ink and transfer paper are transparent, light-colored fabrics make the transferred images show up nicely, whereas dark fabrics don't work at all.*

And inkjet transfers aren't just for T-shirts! Although optimized for 100% cotton and 50/50 cotton/polyester blends, they can be used with any fabric or ready-made item that can withstand the ironing temperature.

You can find inkjet transfer paper in most office supply, computer, and elec-

Heat Transfer Inks

Sawgrass Systems markets dye sublimation heat transfer ink for some Epson desktop inkjet printers. After printing on plain paper with this ink, you can heat-transfer that printout to any surface that has a high polyester content, such as mouse pads and specially coated ceramic mugs and metals. But before you get too excited, I should mention that the cartridges currently cost over $350 each, relegating them to professional use. The samples I've seen are impressive, but I haven't tested the cartridges myself, so I'll stop short of recommending them.

tronics stores, as well as many mail-order catalogs. If you have a choice, get the newer variety of transfer paper that can be peeled after it cools, such as Hanes Easy-Peel. This type of paper is much easier to apply with a household iron than hot peel transfers and gives much better results on coarse or thick fabrics like canvas or sweatshirt fleece.

CAUTION: *Do not use inkjet transfer paper in your printer if your printer has a heating element.*

When working with transfer paper, be sure to print the image reversed so that it will appear correctly on the shirt. Most printers support this reversal, or mirroring, with a "flip horizontal," "back print film," or "mirror image" command in their Print or Page Setup options. If your printer does not have a mirroring option, you can usually flip the design in the program you used to create it. For more details, see page 77.

Because transfer paper is expensive, always test your design on plain paper first. Your plain-paper test will help you catch errors like an unmirrored image element or stray guidelines.

Crafting Tools

Once the computer design, printing, and media are settled, specialized crafting tools (and the techniques to make the best use of them) take center stage. The right tools will make a big difference in what you can do and how easily you can do it.

CUTTING AND PUNCHING

The standard 8 1/2 x 11-inch page is a dead giveaway that you've created your work on a computer, but that's easy enough to remedy. Your basic pair of scissors or trusty hobby knife (such as an X-Acto knife) will be fine for many paper-cutting tasks, but you'll probably want to add a few more cutting tools to your arsenal for special jobs and special effects.

Scoring

With few exceptions, any time your design calls for a fold, you should first *score* the paper (break the top layer of paper fibers) so that it will produce a neater fold and a more professional look. Scoring can be done on either side of the page with anything from a fingernail to the non-cutting edge of a knife blade, depending on your preference. You can also get scoring blades to fit in the rotary cutting systems discussed below.

Perforating

When you *perforate* paper, you make a series of small slots or holes to facilitate easy removal of that section—for a tear-away order form, for instance. Perforating blades are available for the rotary cutting systems discussed below, or use an unthreaded sewing machine with a fine needle and short stitch length to perforate paper or card stock.

Using Decorative Blade Scissors

Choose from dozens of novelty-blade scissors with designs such as zigzags, waves, scallops, notches, flounces, jigsaw look, and deckle edges, among others. They're great for spicing up stationery, magnets, and greeting cards. Use them when layering papers of different colors or when simulating photographs (see Photo Prints project on page 48, Color Plate 3) or postage stamps. Decorative scissors are a "must-have," because nearly every craft project can benefit from their use. Choose a few versatile designs, but be careful! You'll soon want them all.

TIP: If you're having trouble cutting a straight line with decorative scissors, lightly mark your cutting line with a pencil. Then, pick a repeating element on the scissors' pattern, such as the bottom of a wave or the point on a Victorian edge, and make sure that element falls consistently on your penciled guideline.

Paper Trimming

Paper cutters are no longer just for the office. The latest breed of tools for home paper trimming will ensure clean, square edges for your projects at home, too.

Personal Paper Trimmers

I'm sold on the inexpensive little Personal Paper Trimmer from Fiskars. Its sliding blade makes precise straight cuts up to 8 1/2 inches long, including inside cuts (like cutting a rectangular window in the middle of a page). A new, larger model makes cuts up to 12 inches long.

TIP: *Use a paper trimmer to remove the blank edges from your page and create a full bleed design (that is, with no unprinted margins). You won't believe how much this one little technique will improve the look of your projects.*

Desktop Paper Trimmers

For cutting multiple sheets or making longer cuts, move up to a guillotine- or rotary-style paper trimmer. Fixtures in most offices, guillotine-style trimmers have a pivoting blade arm that swings down to cut the paper.

In contrast, rotary trimmers have round blades that roll along a fixed track. Although less powerful than guillotine trimmers, rotary trimmers are considerably safer. Both feature a work surface of up to 12 x 24 inches and a grid that helps with measurement and alignment.

If you choose the rotary trimmer from Fiskars, you get the added benefit of nine optional blade styles besides the straight blade. Decorative ones include pinking, "Victorian," wave, deckle, "squiggle," scallop, and "tiara." All

can cut several layers of paper or card stock; the straight, pinking, and wave blades can cut fabric, cardboard, and vinyl as well. Two specialty wheels handle scoring and perforating, respectively.

TIP: *To make it easier to see the cut line when using a desktop rotary trimmer, lay a piece of opaque, low-tack tape over the length of the cutting mat strip so that the blade will slice it in two lengthwise. Cut the tape and then remove one-half of it. The cut edge of the tape remaining on your mat shows you exactly where the blade will fall.*

Using Handheld Rotary Cutters

The decorative blades that come with the Fiskars Desktop Rotary Trimmer also fit the Fiskars 45 mm Rotary Cutter, which looks similar to a pizza slicer. With the handheld cutter and a cutting mat, you can make smooth cuts guided by a rigid template or paper pattern.

No matter what your preference, either a desktop or handheld rotary cutter will make a valuable addition to your gadget collection. Together they make a flexible system capable of handling nearly every trimming, edging, scoring, or perforating task you'll run across. Somewhat of a hybrid is the Fiskars Craft and Quilting Cutter, which consists of a rolling blade carriage mounted to a 24-inch-long acrylic ruler.

Circle Cutting

The ability to cut perfect circles will greatly expand your computer craft options. The good news is that a sharp knife and a steady hand are not the only way to do it; special-duty cutters are the answer. For example, fixed-diameter cutters, like Badge-A-Minit's handy Cut-a-Circle, will cut circles to fit button forms in two sizes—2 1/4 or 2 3/4 inches in diameter. Of course, you can use it for more than just buttons.

Fully adjustable circle cutters, available in several styles, adjust to cut any diameter within a certain range. The styles found in scrapbooking stores are versatile because they do not damage the center portion of the item being cut, but they can be expensive. Art and drafting supply houses carry inexpensive compass-style cutters, like the Olfa CMP-1 Compass Cutter, which leaves the paper circle with a pinhole in the middle from the compass point. Even with this limitation, I get a lot of use from mine and recommend it.

Decorative Punching

Hole punchers are nothing new, but the last few years have seen the appearance of a whole range of specialty punches. Small tabletop *craft punches* make holes shaped like apples, teddy bears, houses, dinosaurs, and lots more. Several sizes are available to punch shapes up to about 1 1/4 inches across.

Border punches are the latest addition to the craft punch lineup, made especially for adding decorative flourishes, like an Aztec pattern, along the edges of your page, or to create evenly spaced holes for threading ribbon.

Handheld punches that look like what we used in grade school are another variation of craft punches, but instead of the standard holes, these punch miniature circles, stars, hearts, and other designs from 1/8 to 1/4 inch across. Experienced paper crafters combine these punches to produce spectacular lace-like patterns.

A simple cut-out can add interest to any page, but not without some advance planning; its placement is con-

strained by the "reach" and orientation of your punch. Curiously, most craft punches orient their designs to work from the bottom of the page, so you can't, for instance, punch a row of cats across the top of the page—unless you want upside-down cats!

TIP: *When punching thin material, sandwich it between two sheets of scrap paper to prevent the edges from tearing or bending and produce a cleaner cut.*

How about these punching ideas?

- Use the little paper shapes that are the by-products of punching to create more unique products. Brightly colored or metallic paper, for example, yields eye-catching confetti. Print on the paper before punching for further customization (see our Custom Confetti project, page 90, Color Plate 24).

- When you start with adhesive stock, the punching process naturally yields ready-made stickers. Stickers are a great way to work around the punch-reach, orientation, and background constraints of directly punching your original. For instance, instead of punching out cats from a blue page and putting yellow paper behind the opening, just use yellow cat stickers and you can put them anywhere you like.

Die Cutting

Wouldn't it be great if we could die-cut large shapes other than circles and rectangles from our printouts? Unfortunately, the equipment for this costs hundreds of dollars—a little steep even for the most enthusiastic computer crafter. But you can print on ready-made die-cut shapes with a simple piggyback technique we describe in the Die-Cut Gift Tag project on page 86, Color Plate 22.

Corner Rounding

Rounding the corners of your pages is a small touch that makes a big difference. You can do it with either a punch or scissors designed especially for the task. In addition to simple rounding like we used in our Checkbook Cover project on page 70, Color Plate 14, you'll find at least a dozen other specially designed corner tools to produce looks from fun to sophisticated like our Bottle Label project on page 94, Color Plate 26.

EMBELLISHMENT

People say you can tell a computer crafter by the glitter on her keyboard, but glitter is only one way to embellish a printout.

Adding Dimension

Anything that adds depth to an otherwise flat piece makes a more interesting craft. Clever folding and the addition of pop-ups are some bold ways to do this, but there are many other ways, too.

Powder Embossing

Powder embossing is a technique you can use to create an interesting raised effect in your designs. To do it, apply your base image with a rubber stamp, embossing pen, or inkjet printer. While the ink is still wet, pour a special powder over it and tap away any powder that doesn't stick to the wet ink. You then heat the page so that the remaining powder melts, bonding to the paper and creating the raised effect. There are dozens of powder colors and special effects available, including clear, iridescent, glittering, and even glow-in-the-dark, that allow you to achieve a number of different looks. We used white powder to "print" on black paper in the White-on-Black Design project on page 88, Color Plate 23.

TIP: To powder emboss directly on wet inkjet printouts, you will need to slow the drying process by either printing on some sort of plastic film or by using black ink, if your printer can use pigment-based ink.

A side benefit of powder embossing is that the embossing powder bonds to the paper and is permanent, even if the underlying ink isn't.

Powder embossing is a perfect complement to many inkjet projects. One technique is to hand-color areas to be embossed with slow-drying pens or markers designed specifically for use in powder embossing. You can also use glue pens and heat-resistant high-tack double-sided tape (such as Wonder Tape or Magic Tape). Powder embossing supplies are available at rubber stamp stores, craft stores, and some stationery and bookstores.

Paper Tole

Toling is the art of making three-dimensional scenes from layered paper cutouts. Pieces are mounted with double-sided foam tape or thick adhesive dots so that they stand out from the page and from each other to give the piece varying depths. An example is shown in our Paper Tole Card on page 118, Color Plate 38.

More 3-D Accents

Briefly, here are some other techniques that you can use to give your projects added dimension:

- *Flocking,* which gives your image a fuzzy coating, and Liquid Appliqué, a type of paint that puffs when heated, are two more techniques that add texture and dimension to your projects. We use Liquid Appliqué in one of the Traditional Greeting Cards on page 72, Color Plate 15. For more detailed information on these techniques, check out rubber stamping resources.

- *Paper corrugators* (available in rubber stamp and scrapbooking stores) can take a flat printed piece and give it a dramatic look by adding the trademark hills and valleys of corrugation.

- You can attach all kinds of real-life items to your projects to add instant dimension and bring automatic smiles. Try sand, adhesive bandages, cocktail umbrellas, buttons, charms, bows, diaper pins, rice, fishing lures, golf tees, money, candy, personal memorabilia, or whatever strikes your fancy.

- *Shaker* or *water cards* are great novelty items that are always well received. They include small objects that are free to rattle around under a transparent window or float in a bag of water or gel. You can see one example in the Shaker Card project on page 120, Color Plate 39. Use your imagination here to come with some really inventive ideas!

Adding Sparkle

Ever popular among traditional crafters, *glitter pens, glitter glue,* and *glitter sprays* can be used to create highlights or to add overall sparkle to your computer-generated projects, too.

For flashy metallic accents, choose either *craft foil* (found in rubber stamp stores) or *laser color foil* (sold at office supply stores and in desktop publishing catalogs). Craft foil, which comes in various metallic colors and patterns, sticks to glue or double-sided tape you apply to the page and leaves a metallic layer behind when the foil's thin backing is peeled away.

Laser color foil will also work with tape and glue like craft foil, but it is made with a higher-tech use in mind. Laser foil magically sticks to dry laser or copier toner, but not to blank areas of the page, when heat and pressure are applied. This is done in a second pass through a laser printer or photocopier or with a laminating machine. Laser foil comes in various metallic colors and holographic patterns as well as many glossy and matte-finish colors.

Chapter

6

More Techniques for Computer Crafting

Once your project has been printed, trimmed, and embellished, there are various finishing steps you can take to complete and protect it. We'll look at these, as well as some creative ways to craft with inkjet-printed patterns and masters.

SEALING

As wonderful as today's inkjet printers are, they do have some limitations, the most significant of which is that their inks fade and run. Inkjet images are easily degraded by moisture and bright light and must be protected if they are to survive any outdoor or long term use. Here are some ways to do so.

Spray Coating

Some spray coatings will help protect your inkjet printouts. Artists' *fixative*, for instance, gives light-duty protection and won't alter the look of your piece. To prevent inks from running or smearing, apply a layer of fixative to your paper or fabric printouts before using brush-on coatings, such as decoupage medium. I usually spray it on as a first layer under other spray coatings, too.

Clear acrylic sprays, available in matte and glossy finishes, provide the next level of protection and some even block ultraviolet rays in addition to providing water resistance. Glossy sprays will produce glossy results on glossy-finish paper but won't add much, if any, gloss to plain paper. This means you really don't need both kinds—just buy glossy spray.

Lamination

When your project demands more protection than sprays will afford, consider *lamination*, which covers your creation with a layer of plastic or encases it between two layers. Your choices range from package sealing tape and pressure-sensitive laminating sheets to laminating machines. We use two types of lamination in our Bookmark project (page 68, Color Plate 13) and in our Marker Board project (page 50, Color Plate 4).

Here are some lamination options:

* *Pressure-sensitive clear cover* (such as Con-Tact brand) or *laminating sheets* provide good protection for your printouts and give a finished appearance.

* Don't overlook *clear package sealing tape* for small sealing jobs. (For moist environments, overlap your film or tape around the outside of your project to seal the edges so that water will not seep in.)

* *Hot lamination* (wherein you place your project in a plastic pouch and then run it through a laminating machine) gives the best protection and most professional look to your work. It is also a great way to add stiffness to a page.

- Use special pouches with UV protection to help slow the fading of inkjet prints exposed to sunlight.

- Card-size *laminating machines* are inexpensive, but limited to only projects of about 4 inches or less in width. Fortunately, full page-size laminators are becoming more and more affordable.

- Most office supply stores, print shops, and even some craft stores will laminate your 8 1/2 x 11-inch page for about $1.00 per page, so if your needs are limited, this might be your best option.

- Laminating pouches can be sealed with a household iron.

- Recently introduced cold (or tape) laminating machines from Xyron and 3M are an interesting alternative, applying laminating film from rolls onto your page without heat or electricity. These machines can also apply an adhesive layer to the back of your document.

- For sealing fabric, try *iron-on vinyl*, sold in rolls at fabric stores. One drawback is that it leaves a slightly glossy sheen and affects the feel of the fabric—making it slicker and stiffer.

BINDING

When your projects call for binding pages, you can call on several common office techniques. Many binders and report covers require no special equipment to use, although they aren't terribly exciting. Stapling may be a little better if you use a nice custom cover; you can even get colored staples for a tiny flourish.

Plastic comb or *spiral binding* is a simple yet professional answer for binding projects like cookbooks and calendars. Most office supply stores and copy shops provide comb binding for as little as $1.00 per bound book. Better yet, some leave a comb-binding machine accessible so you can do it yourself.

Perfect binding is the method used to bind paperback books. In the desktop rendition, pages are inserted into a ready-made cover with glue and the ensemble is then placed in a perfect-binding machine such as Avery's First Impression models. The machine heats and melts the glue inside the cover. When the glue cools, it holds the pages in place.

Unfortunately, these binding machines and covers are expensive, and cover choices are limited (to 8 1/2 x 11 inches, for instance). Although office supply stores may offer this type of binding, you can do it at home cheaply if you wish. The clever folk at *Flash Magazine* have figured out a way to perfect-bind volumes using their own desktop-printed covers, a hot glue gun, and a frying pan. No kidding! I've adapted their technique for binding a single volume; you'll find instructions for it in the Paperback Book project on page 124, Color Plate 40.

More "crafty" binding techniques include novelty ideas, such as stitching the pages together with a sewing machine or lacing them along with everything from buttons to macaroni, to add a creative flair.

Padding is a remarkably easy process that lets you add professional-looking notepads to your repertoire. See our Notepads project, page 84, Color Plate 21, for an example.

USING ADHESIVES

In the course of completing various craft projects, you'll inevitably need to attach one thing to another. Here are some different ways to do so.

- For paper to paper, the common glue stick works nicely. Adhesive transfer applicators, such as Tombo MonoAdhesive, are a neater but more expensive alternative. Both glue sticks and adhesive applicators come in permanent and removable versions.

- Glue pens, such as the Sailor Rolling Ball, apply glue precisely—especially helpful in small areas.

- Add spray glue, such as 3M Spray Mount Artist's Adhesive, to your shopping list and use it when you need complete and even coverage all the way to the edge of your page. (You can use most glue pens and adhesive sprays as either permanent or repositionable adhesive, depending on the way you apply them. Instructions are on the label.)

- Adhesive-backed magnets or hook-and-loop tape (such as Velcro brand tape) are great for reusable attachments or for convenient mounting of your project once it's done.

- For attaching fabric to fabric or even to paper, fusible (iron-on) adhesive, such as Heat-n-Bond, sold by the yard or in packages at fabric and craft stores, gives great results.

USING INSERT PRODUCTS

A whole class of practical products lets you turn a computer printout into something useful—in a snap. Empty plastic button shells, key rings, mugs, pencil holders, coasters, napkin rings, clocks, and planters are but a few examples of "containers" you decorate by inserting your own artwork. We feature two of these in our Tape Measure and Clock projects (pages 64 and 106; Color Plates 11 and 32). Cut your printout to fit and snap it in for instant giftware.

Media covers with see-through outer pockets (like videotape cases and three-ring binders) are easy to customize by simply slipping in your own design. The same goes for clear vinyl business-card holders and checkbook covers (like the one we use in our Checkbook Cover project on page 70; Color Plate 14).

Fabric stores carry a variety of products, like buttons and barrettes, that are made to be covered with fabric for a coordinated look. Imagine how unique they will be with your very own custom-printed fabric!

USING PATTERNS AND MASTERS

All the techniques we've talked about up to this point involve putting inkjet ink onto a surface either directly or through heat transfer. When neither of those options are possible, or when you don't want the ink to show, you can still use your printout as a pattern or master.

Several crafting techniques won't work with inkjet printouts, but they will work with photocopies. To use these techniques, make a photocopy of an inkjet master. Because public photocopy machines are so readily available and inexpensive to use, this opens up possibilities such as using laser foil and water slide decal film.

Transfer medium (sold under the trade names Picture This or Transfer-It), is an inexpensive way to transfer a black-and-white or color photocopy of any image, including your inkjet-printed ones, to fabric without heat or special equipment. Using this glue-like substance takes several days to complete and is a little messy, but it's a viable alternative in cases where heat transfers cannot be easily applied. Simply follow the instructions on the bottle.

Here are some ways to use inkjet-printed patterns to solve a variety of arts and crafts challenges:

- If you don't have inkjet transfer paper, or want to maintain the fabric feel that is lost with other transfer methods, print just an outline of your design on plain paper. Color in the outlines with transfer pens or transfer crayons (from a craft or fabric store) and iron the image onto the fabric according to package instructions. If you're concerned about the inkjet-printed outlines accidentally transferring to the fabric, print the outline in mirror image on thin paper or vellum and color on the back side of the page instead.

- Print an outline or positioning guide on the back side of your paper or fabric to serve as a guide for cutting or punching. Another variation is to tape a printed outline behind a transparent surface to use as a pattern for painting.

- Print the outline or silhouette for a simple image onto card stock. Cut the image out of the page to create stencils for various art projects.

- To cut shapes out of non-printable materials like craft foam or compressed sponge, print the shape at the proper size on plain paper to use as a guide. Lay the paper pattern on top of the material you want to shape and cut through both layers with scissors. Or you can use the pattern to prick tiny holes that will mark your cut line.

- Print an image or outline on transparency film to project it onto another surface or to use as an exposure mask.

These projects will show you how to use both your equipment and knowledge to produce exciting, quality crafts you can be proud of. They were chosen primarily to introduce you to a broad array of media, materials, tools, and techniques with as little repetition as possible. Therefore, I don't necessarily show the very best way to make a particular item. For instance, I detail only one way to make a bookmark, although you could use many other ways (and produce more interesting bookmarks) with procedures you'll find in other projects.

Please use these projects as springboards for your own creations: Mix and match materials and techniques as you follow your imagination.

2

Part 2 **Projects**

About the Instructions

I wrote these instructions assuming that you have a working knowledge of your own software, computer, and printer, and that you've read Chapters 1–6 of this book. The steps are general enough so that you can complete these projects with whatever software you have.

You may need to refer to your software or printer manuals to learn exactly how to perform certain steps, such as setting print options, specifying margins, changing text attributes, mirroring an image, duplicating elements, and so on. Also, remember that your screen may look completely different than the one shown, depending on the software and printer you use.

Because the term for designating print quality varies from printer to printer, I've chosen to use the following terms as standards:

Highest The best quality available for the media type you're using.

Normal The midrange choice, just above draft quality.

Draft The lowest quality, sometimes called Fast or Economy.

Some Words to the Wise

- The instructions that follow are meant to leave plenty of room for your creativity. For instance, you may readily exchange all sorts of clip art, photographs, and stylized text with each other to create your own effects.

- To avoid unpleasant surprises, read through all of the steps carefully before you begin a project.

- Please don't take shortcuts with drying time. Adequate drying time is essential to a successful project—a fact I learned the hard way.

- As with all crafts, you will need a suitable work area and should follow all safety procedures in product instructions. For example, spray adhesives and coatings should be applied in a well-ventilated area away from heat sources.

- Though all of these projects can be enjoyed as a family activity, they were not designed for children to accomplish on their own. At a minimum, adult supervision is advised for any cutting, spraying, or powder embossing.

I've listed the materials required for each project, but I assume that you always have the following on hand for all projects:

- appropriate clip art and fonts

- a pencil and paper to make notes

- plain paper for draft printing

- newspaper to protect surfaces from overflow of sprays, glitter, and so on

- a cutting mat to protect surfaces from sharp tools

- a ruler

Unless otherwise specified, all "plain, coated, or inkjet paper" is 8 1/2 x 11 inches or A4 size.

1. Gift Wrap

Figure 1. Maximize print area by typing in the minimum margin values your printer will support, as shown in this example from ClarisWorks.

Figure 2. To change the font, first select the text, then choose a new font from the menu as shown in this example from ClarisWorks.

Turn plain paper into colorful custom gift wrap in a matter of minutes.

WHAT TO DO

1. Open a new document and, under Document Layout, Document Setup, or Page Setup, set the margins for the top, bottom, left, and right sides of the page to the minimum allowable (see Figure 1). Try setting them to zero first. If your program won't accept this setting, use the minimum margin values from your printer worksheet or trial-and-error to set the smallest margins you can—you'll want to print across as much of the paper as you can so that you end up with the largest possible sheet of printed gift wrap.

2. Type in a short message to appear on the printed paper (like "Happy Birthday, Uncle Bill!") and select a font and color to match the occasion, as shown in Figures 2 and 3.

3. Choose the text size based on the size of the gift you will be wrapping, so the message will be easy to read on the finished package. The smaller the gift, the smaller the font.

4. Make five to ten additional copies of the message using your software's cut-and-paste features, changing the font and color with each repetition.

5. Once you've filled a good-sized block of text with varied fonts and colors, cut and paste it until you fill the entire page with type and color.

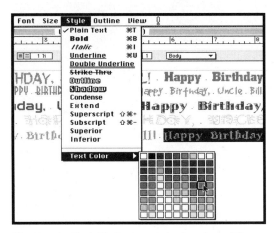

Figure 3. In ClarisWorks, text color is selected from a palette at the bottom of the Style menu.

TIP: To get rid of the jagged right edge, select full justification from the text alignment choices. Figure 4 shows before and after views.

6. Print your finished "gift wrap" using the highest quality setting available.

7. If desired, trim off the unprinted margins when you wrap the package, or simply fold them under as you wrap.

ABOUT THE SAMPLE (COLOR PLATE 1)

The birthday wrap was prepared in ClarisWorks (word-processing module) using fun display fonts and bright colors. It was printed at high resolution on coated inkjet paper. The package was wrapped with the paper turned diagonally for a more interesting look.

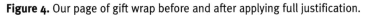

Figure 4. Our page of gift wrap before and after applying full justification.

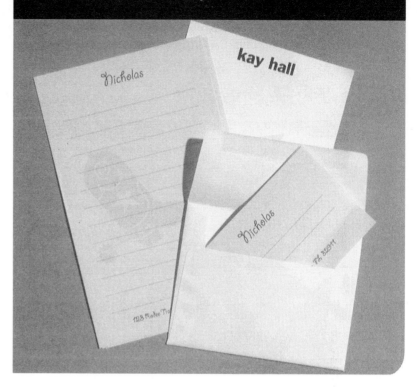

Print two sheets of lined or unlined personal stationery side by side with your choice of lettering and a printed "watermark" in the background.

WHAT TO DO

1. Open a new document in wide or landscape orientation.

2. Set the left and right margins to 0.6 inch and the top and bottom margins to 0.5 inch.

3. Set up two columns on your page with 1.2 inches between them. The column setting will often be found under Layout, Guides, or Format options.

4. Design your stationery on one-half of the page, using only one of the columns. When you are satisfied with the design, copy it onto the other half, as shown in Figure 1.

    TIP: *Before duplicating designs containing multiple elements, it is helpful to temporarily "glue" them together using the Group command.*

DIGITAL WATERMARKING

To create a watermark—a graphic that appears faintly behind your design—first set its color to 5 to 10 percent black or equivalent shade of gray as shown in Figure 3. This is also called *screening*. To place it in the background under your other type and art elements, use the Send to Back or similar command, usually under the Arrange menu.

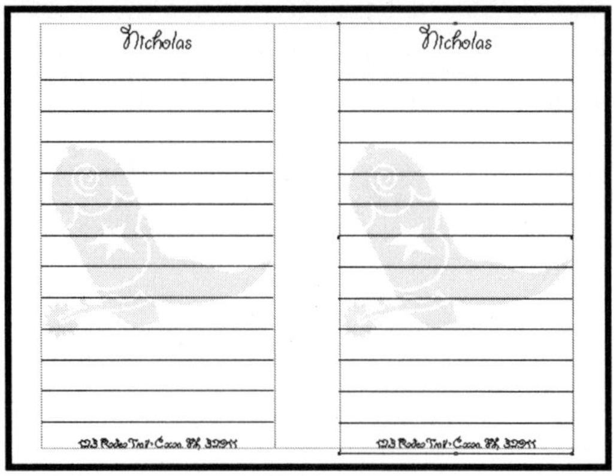

Figure 1. Design the stationery on the left half of the page and copy it to the right half.

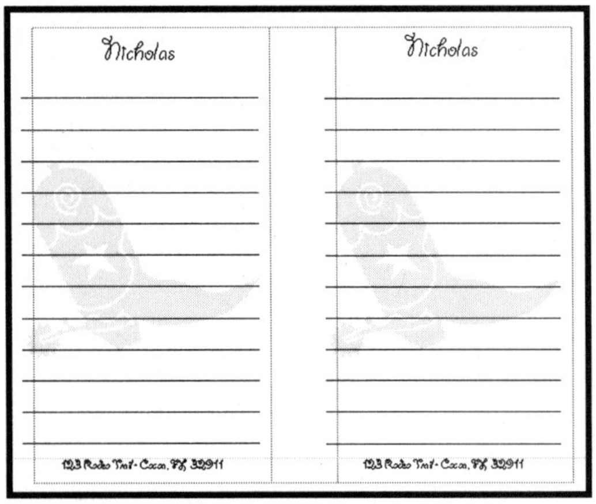

Figure 2. Our software and printer required that we shift our design to the left.

Figure 3. Setting the color of the watermark image in Adobe PageMaker.

5. Print a copy on plain paper in draft mode to check centering and adjust your document on screen as necessary. Figure 2 shows how we had to shift our original design to the left.

6. Print the final copies using the highest quality setting available.

7. Neatly cut the page in half with a paper trimmer to separate the stationery sheets. Bundle with envelopes.

ABOUT THE SAMPLE (COLOR PLATE 2)

The child's stationery shown here was printed in grayscale on colored paper. A Western theme font and matching boot (a dingbat character from the same font) "watermark" make up the simple design, done with desktop publishing software. Hairline-width parallel lines were added to the writing area with the Rule feature.

Special media and decorative edging give your inkjet-printed photographs an authentic look.

WHAT TO DO

1. Scan in or load a digitized photograph from disk and edit as desired. (See the Color Management section in Chapter 1 for tips on photo printing.) This may include cropping or resizing (see Figure 1).

2. Print your photo using your printer's highest quality setting and allow it to dry thoroughly (overnight is best).

3. Spray your print with a protective coating (fixative or matte-finish spray for matte-finish photo paper, glossy-finish spray for glossy-finish photo paper) and allow it to dry.

4. Cut your print roughly to size, then trim its edges with decorative scissors, leaving white margins if desired to give it that olde-time look.

ABOUT THE SAMPLE (COLOR PLATE 3)

These photos were shot with a digital camera, downloaded into the computer, edited, and printed on glossy-finish photo paper. The edges were trimmed using a variety of tools, including Fiskars deckle blade in their desktop rotary trimmer and an Olfa handheld rotary wave cutter.

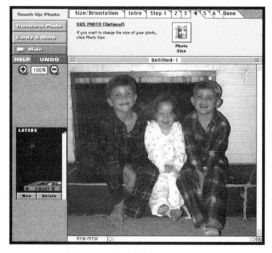

Figure 1. Preparing to resize a photo in Adobe PhotoDeluxe.

Access to pouch-laminating machine

Coated paper (not glossy) or light card stock

Four 1-inch-square pieces of adhesive-backed magnetic sheet

One letter size laminating pouch (heavy duty is best)

One pair medium-duty adhesive-backed hook-and-loop fastener dots (such as Velcro)

One wet-erase pen (the kind used for overhead transparencies)

4. Marker Board

Creative publishing suite

Desktop publishing

Drawing

Photo editing

Hot lamination transforms a full-page border design into a wet-erase marker board, useful for the home or office.

WHAT TO DO

1. Open a one-page document and add art and lettering around the edges to create a decorative, personalized border. The center section of the page should be empty (as in Figure 1) or have a simple, light-colored background, because this is where notes will be written on the marker board.

2. Print a proof copy on plain paper to check for correct centering and other design details. Adjust your design as necessary. (You may trim the final page slightly to center it if desired.)

Figure 1. A marker board design with an open center.

3. Print the final copy on your chosen paper or light card stock using the highest quality setting available and allow the ink to dry.

4. Center the printed page in the laminating pouch, run the pouch through the laminating machine, and allow it to cool.

5. Attach a magnetic square on the back of the board at each corner so that the board can be hung on a refrigerator or filing cabinet.

6. To finish, attach the rough (hooked) half of a hook-and-loop dot to the front of the board at the center of one edge, then attach the soft (looped) half to the pen.

ABOUT THE SAMPLE (COLOR PLATE 4)

Our sample was adapted from a Print Shop graphic and printed on heavyweight inkjet-coated paper from P.S. Ink. The corners were rounded with a punch-style corner rounder for a more finished look.

5. Kids' Stickers

Whether you're making stickers for kids or letting them make their own, printable sheets of removable labels are a godsend.

WHAT TO DO

1. Open a template for your sheet of labels, usually by selecting from a list of standard formats (see Figure 1). If your specific label type is not listed, you'll need to modify a similar template or create a new one. See the label's packaging for dimensions and other information that will help you to do so.

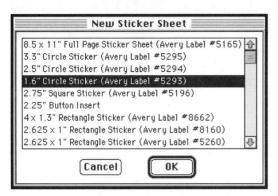

Figure 1. Selecting a sticker format in Sticker Shop.

Figure 2. Designing an individual sticker in Sticker Shop.

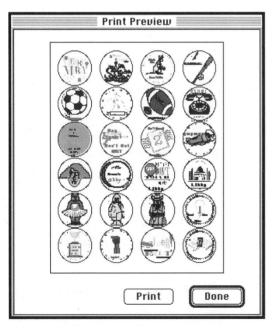

Figure 3. Sticker Shop automatically places stickers in the correct position on the page for printing.

2. Select, import, or create graphics for your stickers and add text if desired, as shown in Figure 2.

3. Create or duplicate the desired number of stickers and arrange them on the page as in Figure 3 or use your software's Tile, Duplicate, or Multiple Copies features to do this automatically.

4. Print a test copy on plain paper to proof. To see whether your printing aligns with the label cuts, hold the printout behind a blank sheet of labels in front of a strong light and look through the printout to the labels. You'll be able to tell if your printing is aligned properly. If not, adjust your design as necessary.

5. Print the final copy of your stickers on label stock using your printer's normal mode.

ABOUT THE SAMPLE (COLOR PLATE 5)

My daughter, age four at the time, created these samples using Sticker Shop from Mindscape. We printed the stickers on 1 2/3-inch round labels from Avery—perfect for mounting on old flipper caps (remember the POG craze?) her brothers had left over!

Printing on ready-made envelopes with an inkjet printer can be a challenge, but by "rolling your own," you can get a foolproof designer envelope to complement your quarter-fold size greeting cards and other stationery.

WHAT TO DO

1. Open a template for a cut-and-fold envelope as shown in Figures 1 and 2 or create your own with the dimensions shown in Figure 3 as starting points.

2. Place design and type elements, including all addresses, in the proper locations on the envelope template as shown in Figure 4.

3. Print a draft copy of your envelope on plain paper, then cut out and fold your draft into a mockup to check that your design is correct. If not, adjust your design as necessary and repeat this step.

4. Print the final copy on plain or coated paper using the highest quality setting available.

5. Cut out and fold your envelope to assemble it, then secure it with a glue stick or any other permanent paper adhesive.

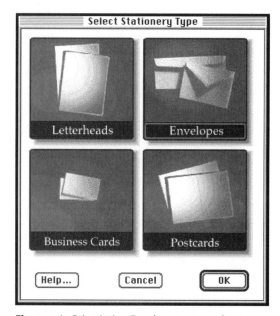

Figure 1. In Print Artist, Envelopes are a subcategory of Stationery.

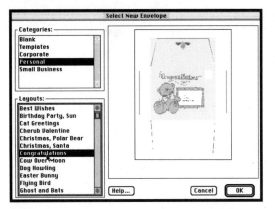

Figure 2. Selecting a predesigned envelope in Print Artist.

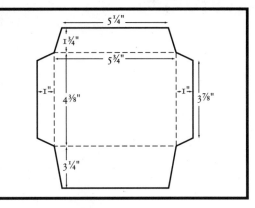

Figure 3. Measurements for making your own announcement-size envelope.

Figure 4. Addressing the cut-and-fold envelope.

6. If you will be mailing your envelope, spray at least the address area with protective coating to help prevent the ink from running in case the envelope gets wet in transit.

ABOUT THE SAMPLE (COLOR PLATE 6)

The envelopes shown here are based on predesigned layouts that come with Stationery Store and Print Artist 4.0. The sealing flaps were trimmed with decorative-edge scissors.

Make your own T-shirt designs look like store-bought screen-printed ones—only better!

WHAT TO DO

1. Prepare a T-shirt design that is no larger than your printable page (see your printer manual or simply use 8 x 10 as the design size). The design may need to be smaller for a child-sized shirt. Keep in mind that the best-looking T-shirts usually have bold graphics, high-contrast color schemes, and large, legible type.

2. Print a draft copy of your design in mirror image as shown in Figure 1 (see How to Print in Mirror Image on page 77) to check for size and other details (to proofread text, hold the page up in front of a bright light and read through the back of the page). Adjust the design as necessary.

3. Print your final copy in mirror image on transfer paper, using the printer settings recommended by the paper's manufacturer.

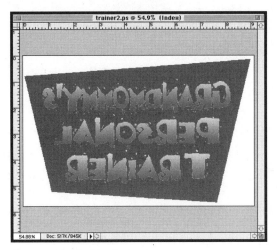

Figure 1. The T-shirt design in a paint program after mirroring.

4. Trim the transfer as close to its printed edges as practical (within manufacturer's recommendations). Applying these unprinted areas of the film to the shirt can detract from your design, especially on shirts other than white—where they are most noticeable.

5. Iron the design onto your T-shirt, peel off the backing, and launder your shirt following the manufacturer's instructions every step of the way.

   NOTE: *Allow a few seconds for your design to cool on the T-shirt before handling.*

ABOUT THE SAMPLE (COLOR PLATE 7)

This transfer, originally designed for a gray T-shirt, uses a full-bleed (edge-to-edge) design to create a professional look. The text was set in a novelty font and colored with a smooth blend from yellow to red (look up Gradients, Blends, or Strata in your software documentation to learn how to do this).

After the transfer was printed, the unprinted portion and the edge of the solid blue background was trimmed with a "ripple" blade loaded in a Fiskars rotary trimmer. Because no unprinted film appears on the shirt, it has the look and feel of screen printing—the technique used by professionals.

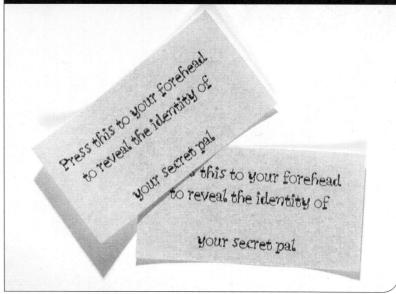

Press this to your forehead to reveal the identity of your secret pal

8. Color Change Hidden Message

A "secret" message lies hidden on this special paper until the heat from a fingertip reveals it. How's that for a magic touch?

WHAT TO DO

1. The trick to working with color change paper is to print the hidden message in a color that matches the paper in its cool state closely enough that the message doesn't show. When the recipient touches the printed area, the paper changes color, but the ink doesn't—so the message seems to magically appear. To determine the matching color you should use, begin with the manufacturer's recommendations, if available, or simply make a guess. Print test phrases or color swatches on the color change paper (see Figure 1) using your printer's highest quality setting and adjust colors until you find one that blends in with the paper when the paper is cool. Then hold the paper to warm it and, when it changes color, be sure that you can see the test printing.

   > **TIP:** *Record the results from your test printing, including the color name or numeric values and the printer settings, and store them with your color change paper for future reference.*

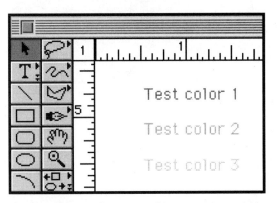

Figure 1. The test document with text set in several different colors.

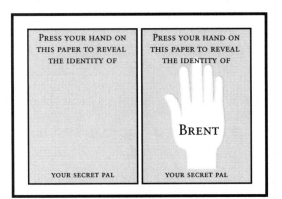

Figure 2. Setting custom colors in Canvas.

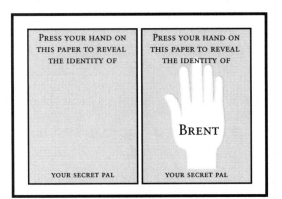

Figure 3. The secret message is revealed!

TIP: *If you have a specialty photo ink cartridge for your printer, load it for this project. It will make pastel color-matching easier.*

2. Prepare your layout and color the text to be hidden with the color determined in Step 1.

3. Print your design onto the color change paper. Be sure to select exactly the same printer settings that yielded the best color match in Step 1. (See Figure 2.)

4. To reveal the hidden message, wait until the ink is dry and run your fingers over the image area to warm the paper as shown in Figure 3.

ABOUT THE SAMPLE (COLOR PLATE 8)

This fun technology is great for revealing mysteries such as the identity of a secret pal (maybe you!). On the blue-to-white color change paper in this sample, I used 5 percent cyan to print the hidden text. When the paper is heated (by a forehead in this case), the message becomes clearly visible against the white background.

Make anyone you love to hate the centerpiece of this portable target printed on opaque cling film. Stick it to the nearest sliding glass door and fire away with soft projectiles such as rubber bands, Nerf balls, or sticky darts.

Figure 1. White circles are drawn over base image.

Figure 2. Dennis Rodman before Kai's Power Goo.

Figure 3. Dennis Rodman after Kai's Power Goo.

WHAT TO DO

1. Choose or design a base image, such as a head-and-shoulders photo, and overlay white (or other contrasting color) concentric circles on it to make a target as shown in Figure 1.

2. Print your design on white window cling film using the highest quality setting available and allow it to dry thoroughly (overnight is best).

3. Trim your printout as desired, leaving at least a small unprinted margin for handling. To use your target, peel away the protective backing and press it lightly onto a clean, smooth surface. Save the backing for storing the target between uses.

ABOUT THE SAMPLE (COLOR PLATE 9)

The image of Dennis Rodman in this sample was created with the help of Kai's Power Goo (see Figures 2 and 3) and imported into a drawing program, where the circles were added.

WHAT YOU NEED

Card stock or perforated business card stock

Paper trimmer

Protective coating spray

Tape measure with business card slot

10. Oversized Poster

RECOMMENDED SOFTWARE

Creative publishing suite

Desktop publishing

Drawing

Photo editing

Copying a master may seem too simple to even list as a project, but many people forget that they can use their inkjet printout as a photocopy master to quickly obtain a permanent image and/or oversized page printing.

WHAT TO DO

1. Determine the optimum size for your poster design based on the size you can print and the size you will have the image enlarged to. To produce the best quality image, the master design should be proportional to the final poster size so that the design fills the poster page and is as large as possible within the page. For instance, if you want to produce an 18 x 24-inch poster from an 8 1/2 x 11-inch inkjet master (assuming an 8 x 10-inch printable area), size your design at 7 1/2 x 10 inches. For an 11 x 17-inch poster, start with 6 1/2 x 10 inches.

Figure 1. Poster design from Print Artist.

2. Design your poster within the size determined in Step 1. Simple bold designs like the one in Figure 1 work best, because posters are generally viewed at a distance.

3. Print a proof copy and check it carefully for typographical errors, centering, and other design details. Keep in mind that the enlargement process will tend to exacerbate flaws in your design. Adjust as necessary.

4. Print the final copy of your image on coated paper using the highest quality setting available and allow it to dry. This will serve as your master. Check it over thoroughly, because errors discovered later could be costly.

5. Enlarge your poster to its final size on a large-format photo-copier. Follow the instructions on the copier or ask for assistance, if necessary, to be sure you place your master in the proper position on the glass the first time.

ABOUT THE SAMPLE (COLOR PLATE 10)

This poster design from Print Artist was enlarged to 18 x 24 inches for less than $3 from an 8 1/2 x 11-inch master. The original image was in color, but I printed it in grayscale mode because the final poster would be black and white.

Card stock or perforated business card stock

Paper trimmer

Protective coating spray

Tape measure with business card slot

11. Tape Measure

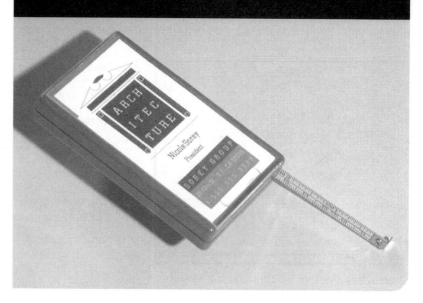

Creative publishing suite

Desktop publishing

Drawing

Specialty products made to hold commercially-printed business cards make great showcases for your inkjet-printed designs, too.

WHAT TO DO

1. Choose a ready-made business card design as shown in Figure 1 or create your own within a 3 1/2 x 2-inch rectangle. If you're not using perforated stock, print crop marks to aid in cutting.

2. Print and trim a draft copy to proof your design and be sure it closely matches the size of a standard business card.

3. Print the final copy of your design using the highest quality setting available and allow the ink to dry thoroughly.

4. Trim the final printed insert to size and spray it with a protective coating.

5. When the spray has dried, install your insert into the tape measure's slot according to the manufacturer's instructions.

Figure 1. Business card design from Print Artist.

This tape measure, manufactured by ProGold, turns an architect's business card into a promotional item the client is sure to hang on to. The card design is from Print Artist.

> **TIP:** *Business card–size designs created as above can also be used in calendars, coasters, letter openers, luggage tags, magnets, paperweights, rotary card sleeves, and visor clips. See Appendix B for sources.*

Paper trimmer (personal size preferred)

Plain or colored paper

Removable adhesive glue stick (such as 3M Post-It) or applicator (such as Tombo MonoAdhesive)

RECOMMENDED SOFTWARE

Creative publishing suite

Desktop publishing

Drawing

12. Sticky Notes

Figure 1. A single blank note design.

Make yourself a handful of custom-printed sticky notes using plain paper and a special adhesive.

WHAT TO DO

1. Lay out the design for a single note, adding your choice of text and graphics as shown in Figure 1. (The note pages can be any size you like.)

2. Add your written message to the design, perhaps in a handwriting-style font, or leave the writing area empty for real handwriting later.

3. Add crop marks or faint guidelines at the edge of the note to aid in cutting (see Figure 2).

Figure 2. A light gray rectangle of hairline width is added as a cutting guide.

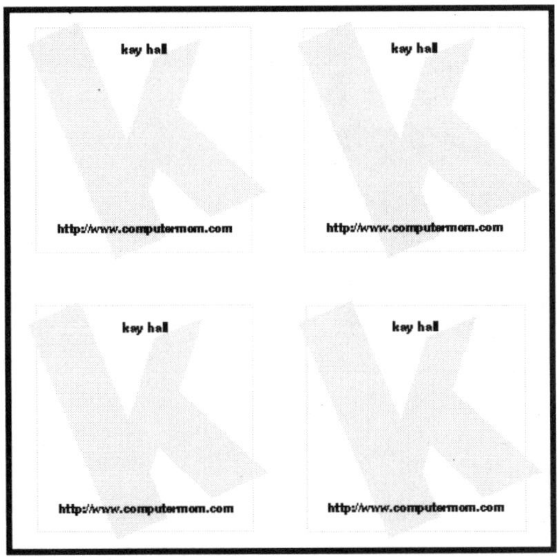

Figure 3. Multiple notes duplicated on the page.

4. Cut and paste, or use your software's Duplicate or Replicate command, to make multiple copies of your design on the page, if desired. See Figure 3.

   TIP: *In most creative publishing suites, multiple copies can be generated automatically when printing by selecting Tile under Print Options.*

5. Print using the highest quality setting available.

6. Trim each note to size following the guidelines you printed in Step 3 above.

7. On the back of each note, apply a stripe of removable adhesive along the top 1/2 inch or so. Allow to dry according to glue instructions.

8. Store your finished notes on a clean laminated surface or waxed paper until they're ready to use.

ABOUT THE SAMPLE (COLOR PLATE 12)

For "authenticity," my notes are printed on yellow paper and cut to 3 x 3-inch size. The large "k" in the background, set to 5 percent black, was intentionally oversized to bleed off the edges once the notes were trimmed.

WHAT YOU NEED

Card stock

Hole punch

Paper trimmer or hobby knife

Self-adhesive laminating sheets or clear cover

Tassel

13. Bookmark

RECOMMENDED SOFTWARE

Creative publishing suite

Desktop publishing

Drawing

Photo editing

Pressure-sensitive laminating sheets and a tassel give this customized bookmark a professional look.

WHAT TO DO

1. Open and edit a bookmark template or design your own. A standard commercial bookmark is roughly 2 x 7 inches, but you can use any size you like.

2. Duplicate the desired number of bookmark designs on the page and edit individual bookmarks as appropriate (see Figure 1).

3. Print a proof copy on plain paper to check design details and adjust as necessary.

4. Print the final copy of your design on card stock using the highest quality setting available.

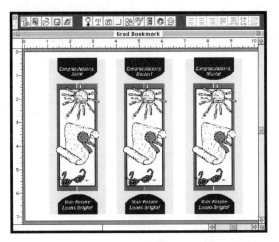

Figure 1. A ready-made bookmark design modified and copied multiple times into a Print Artist sign document.

5. Trim the bookmark design to size.

6. Cover both sides of bookmark with laminating sheet, leaving a 1/4-inch or larger overlapping margin on all sides.

   TIP: If you have a card-size laminating machine, you can laminate bookmarks by cutting letter-size pouches into vertical strips narrow enough to feed through the laminator.

7. Burnish down the laminating film, making sure to seal all edges securely.

8. Trim the plastic around the outside of the bookmark, leaving an even margin of at least 1/8 inch around all edges to resist moisture. (You can trim the film flush with the paper if you wish, but only if you aren't concerned with waterproofing the bookmark.)

9. Punch a hole in the top center of your laminated bookmark and insert the tassel to complete.

ABOUT THE SAMPLE (COLOR PLATE 13)

This graduation bookmark was composed in Print Artist, printed on Micro Format Super Color card stock, and covered with laminating film. Although tassels are normally reserved for more formal designs, adding them here is in keeping with the graduation theme.

Clear vinyl checkbook cover

Corner rounder (optional)

Plain or coated paper or card stock (recommended)

Scissors or paper trimmer (preferred)

Creative publishing suite

Desktop publishing

Photo editing

14. Checkbook Cover

Simply slip your printed design into a clear flexible vinyl cover, like this checkbook-sized one, for a quick and easy personalized gift.

WHAT TO DO

1. Measure your vinyl checkbook cover to determine the size insert you need, then design a template in your software to match, as shown in Figure 1.

    TIP: A Print Artist template for a 6 x 6 1/2-inch checkbook cover insert is available at http://pages.prodigy.com/cathymc/covers.htm.

2. Lay out your text and graphics on the template as shown in Figure 2.

3. Print a draft copy of your design on plain paper, trim it, and be sure it fits properly inside your vinyl cover.

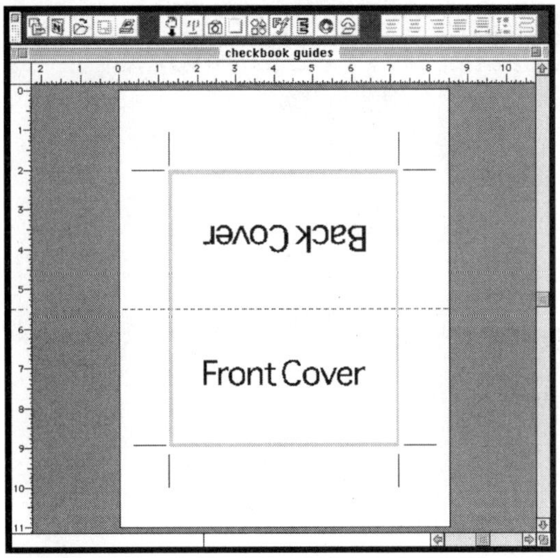

Figure 1. Checkbook template in Print Artist.

Figure 2. Completed checkbook design in Print Artist.

4. Print the final copy of your cover insert on coated paper or card stock using the highest quality setting available.

5. Trim the printout to size, round the corners if you wish, and slip the insert into your plastic checkbook cover.

About the Sample (Color Plate 14)

The image for this checkbook cover was put together in a photo editing program, then imported into Print Artist for placement. It was printed on light card stock, which provides a good balance between flexibility and durability. Rounding the corners provided a better fit as well as a more finished look. Crafty Accessories (see Appendix C for contact information) was the source for both the checkbook cover and the Print Artist template.

> **TIP:** *Follow the same basic steps listed with this project to create inserts for similar vinyl cover projects like photo albums, videocassette cases, three-ring binders, presentation portfolios, and business card holders. See Appendix B for more sources of insert products.*

15. Traditional Greeting Cards

If a card-shop look (or better) is your goal, simple embellishments will get you there.

WHAT TO DO

1. Open a template for a half-fold greeting card layout or create your own.

    TIP: *To make a template for a half-fold card, set up a two-page document and divide each page in half. Generally, your front and inside messages will occupy the same position—but on two separate pages. For a horizontal or top-fold card, place the front of the card on the bottom half of Page 1 and the inside message on the bottom of Page 2. For a vertical or side-fold card, place the front message on the right half of Page 1 and the inside message on the right half of page 2.*

2. Choose a design that lends itself to embellishment (see Embellishments Ideas sidebar on page 73) and edit each panel as desired (see Figure 2).

3. Print a draft copy of Page 1 of your design. When the ink is dry, reload your printout into the printer and print Page 2 on the reverse side of Page 1. Fold the draft as you would a card and check design details. Make corrections as necessary.

4. Print a final copy of your Page 1 design on card stock using the highest quality setting available. When Page 1 is dry, reload the sheet as determined in Step 3 and print Page 2 on the back of it.

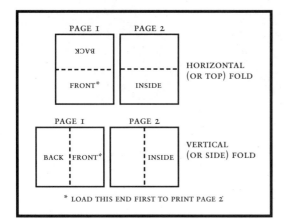

Figure 1. Positioning and printing the front and inside messages for (a) top-fold and (b) side-fold cards.

EMBELLISHMENT IDEAS

Try these embellishment ideas if your image has:

A beach	Glue on real sand.	**Glass**	Adhere a piece of clear laminating film cut to shape.
A bunny tail	Glue on a mini-pompom.		
Clothing or upholstery	Glue on real fabric cut to fit the outline required by your design.	**Snow**	Cover with glitter or Liquid Appliqué.
Eyes	Glue on wiggly eyes.	**Water**	Cover with glitter or clear embossing powder.
Fur	Cover with flocking.		
		Wood	Iron on wood veneer.

Figure 2. A ready-made card design from Print Artist.

TIP: *If you made a template according to Figure 1, reload the page so that the front panel of the card heads into the printer first (blank side down for a front-loading printer and blank side forward for a top-loading printer) in order to print Page 2 in the proper orientation. If you used a ready-made template, follow the instructions that came with it or run a test to determine the correct orientation. In Print Artist, for instance, reload Page 1 with the front panel of the card at the outer end of the input tray. Make a note of the correct loading orientation so you'll have that information for printing your final card—both this time and in future print runs.*

5. Spray the side(s) of your printout that you plan to embellish with fixative and allow that to dry thoroughly.

6. Select areas of the image to highlight and embellish them using a glue pen and glitter, glitter glue, embossing powder, Liquid Appliqué, or flocking according to the package directions.

7. When you've finished embellishing your card and the glue is dry, score, fold, and trim it as desired to complete.

ABOUT THE SAMPLES (COLOR PLATE 15)

The water image on the front of this half-fold anniversary card was first highlighted with a glue pen, then sprinkled with Prisma glitter to make it sparkle. The other sample card shown in Color Plate 15 (with children skiing) was printed on quarter-fold deckle-edge inkjet greeting card paper from Strathmore. The snow on the trees was dabbed with Liquid Appliqué, left to dry overnight, and then heated to make it puff up.

Finished (store-bought or homemade) wooden plaque base

Glossy-finish acrylic spray

Inkjet-compatible metallic paper

Paper trimmer or hobby knife

Rubber cement

16. Metallic-Look Plaque

Creative publishing suite

Desktop publishing

Drawing

Photo editing

A face plate printed on metallic inkjet paper tops a blank wooden plaque base to create a dazzling award.

WHAT TO DO

1. Measure the front of your plaque base to determine the maximum size for your design. Make your design area proportionally smaller if you want to leave a wood "margin" showing around the "metal" face plate. See Figure 1.

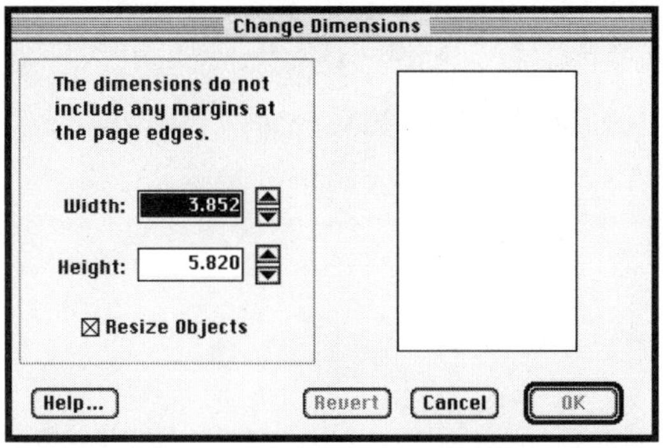

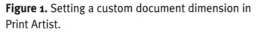

Figure 1. Setting a custom document dimension in Print Artist.

Figure 2. "Metal" face plate layout in Print Artist.

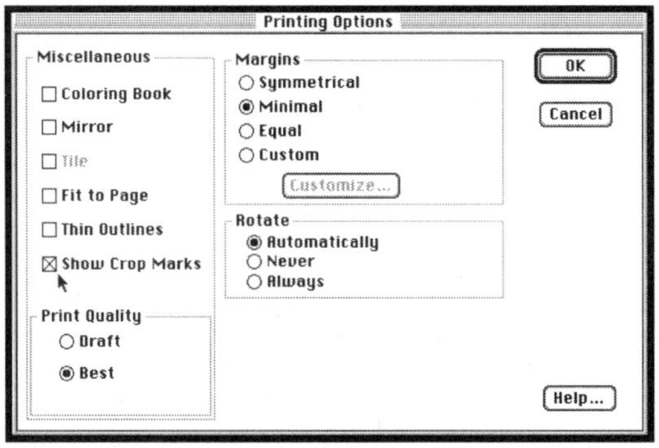

Figure 3. Print Artist set to print crop marks automatically.

2. Lay out your text and graphics and add crop marks, if desired, to aid in cutting as shown in Figures 2 and 3.

3. Load metallic paper into your printer and print on it according to the manufacturer's instructions. Allow it to dry thoroughly (overnight is best).

4. Spray your finished design with glossy-finish acrylic to give it extra protection and shine. Allow it to dry thoroughly. Finally, cut it to size and use rubber cement to glue it onto the wooden base.

ABOUT THE SAMPLE (COLOR PLATE 16)

I intentionally chose a rectangular wood plaque base so that I could make clean matching cuts with a personal paper trimmer. I created the layout in Print Artist using a graphic and fonts included with the software.

Adhesive-backed holographic film

Inkjet-compatible transparency film

> **NOTE:** *Holo-Graf-Craft Kit from D. Brooker and Associates may be substituted for above items.*

Hobby knife or personal paper trimmer

RECOMMENDED SOFTWARE

Creative publishing suite

Desktop publishing

Drawing

Photo editing

17. Holographic Business Cards

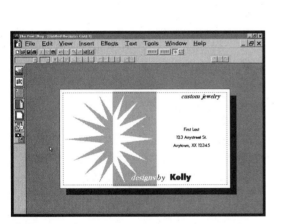

Figure 1. A ready-made business card design in Print Shop Premier.

Reverse printing on transparency film is the clever secret behind these striking and durable business cards.

WHAT TO DO

1. Create a business card template (standard size is 3 1/2 x 2 inches) or open a ready-made design as shown in Figure 1. Add desired graphics and text for name, address, and phone information.

2. Duplicate the desired number of cards on the page (if your software won't do so automatically when printing—see Figure 2) and print a proof on plain paper. Check your proof for typographical errors or any other problems and correct them as necessary.

Figure 2. Print Shop automatically prints a page of cards.

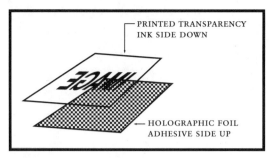

PRINTED TRANSPARENCY
INK SIDE DOWN

HOLOGRAPHIC FOIL
ADHESIVE SIDE UP

Figure 3. Apply holographic foil to the reverse-printed side of the film.

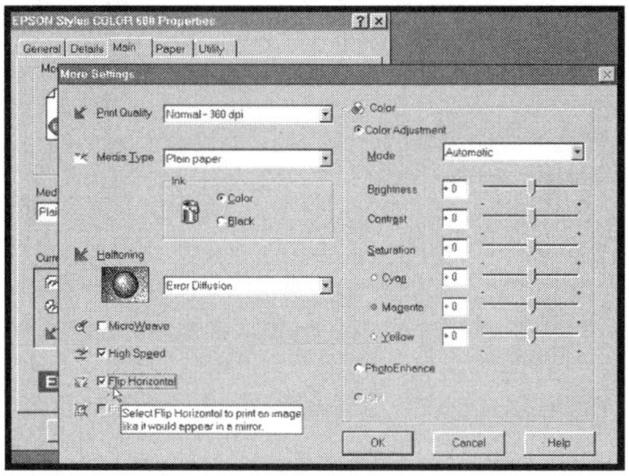

Figure 4. Flip horizontal checkbox in Epson printer properties dialog.

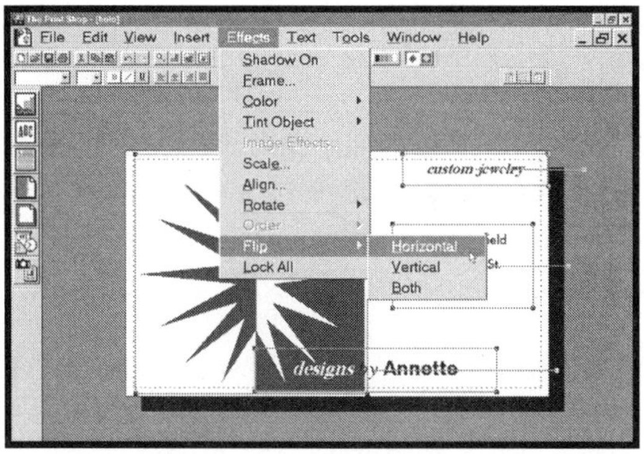

Figure 5. The Flip horizontal command in Paint Shop Premier.

HOW TO PRINT IN MIRROR IMAGE

Most new printers have an option to reverse the entire page by selecting Mirror Image or Flip Horizontal under Print or Page Setup (see Figure 4), or by choosing Back Print Film or T-Shirt Transfer Paper in the Media Options (see Figure 1-5 on page 7). Some programs, such as Print Artist and Print Shop Premier, add a mirroring or flip horizontal function under their own Print Options. (See Figure 1-7 on page 8.)

If your printer does not have mirror image capabilities, you can usually flip images in the program you use to create them. To do this, group your design, then check the various menu options for one that mirrors the selected image (see Figure 5).

As a last resort, you can take a screen shot of your image and reverse it in a paint program, such as Windows Paint, but this method will limit your image resolution to your monitor's resolution.

3. Print another draft on plain paper, this time with the design reversed (see "How to Print a Mirror Image" above), and use this draft to verify that mirroring was successful.

4. Print the final copy in reverse on transparency film, using the highest quality printer setting available.

5. Allow your print out to dry at least overnight, then back the printed side of the film with holographic film according to the manufacturer's instructions. See Figure 3.

6. Trim the cards to size to finish.

ABOUT THE SAMPLE (COLOR PLATE 17)

This neat idea was the brainchild of Dennis Brooker of D. Brooker and Associates, and we used his holographic film for our cards. The layout is included with Print Shop Premier 5.0.

WHAT YOU NEED

Adhesives safe for framing fabric

Batting (one piece at least as large as the mat opening)

Fixative spray

One piece of stiff cardboard to fit the frame

Picture frame and matching size mat

Ready-to-print fabric sheets or inkjet-coated satin finish fabric

Scissors

RECOMMENDED SOFTWARE

Creative publishing suite

Desktop publishing

Drawing

Photo editing

No time for needlework? Use fabric printing and a clever framing trick to simulate it instead.

WHAT TO DO

1. Choose one of three ways to digitize an embroidered design: (1) Scan a finished cross-stitch or other embroidery as shown in Figure 1, (2) simulate it with a pattern of x's to form your design, or (3) type a sentiment with a stitch font.

   TIP: A fourth way for committed crafters: Some embroidery software, like Pattern Maker for Cross Stitch from Hobby-Ware, can print in a mode that simulates the look of stitches. You can even import photos and have them converted to stitch patterns, giving you an unlimited supply of "faux cross-stitch" graphics.

2. Scale your design as desired to fit the mat and print a draft copy on plain paper to proof. Adjust the design as necessary.

3. Load a fabric sheet into your printer (see Making Your Own Ready-to-Print Fabric with Freezer Paper on page 79 if you need to prepare fabric for printing) and print your design in normal mode. Allow the ink to dry overnight, then spray with fixative and allow the fixative to dry.

Figure 1. Scan of embroidery enhanced in Adobe PhotoDeluxe.

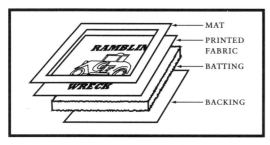

MAT
PRINTED FABRIC
BATTING
BACKING

Figure 2. Place the mat over your printed design; insert batting to plump up fabric.

MAKING YOUR OWN READY-TO-PRINT FABRIC WITH FREEZER PAPER

If you don't want to purchase ready-to-print fabric, you can make your own. To do so, choose a thin, woven, cotton fabric such as muslin or percale. Prewash the fabric to remove any sizing, then iron it thoroughly to eliminate wrinkles. Cut the fabric and freezer paper into sections slightly larger than your final page size. For instance, for a final page size of 8 1/2 x 11 inches, you might cut a 12-inch length of 18-inch-wide freezer paper from the roll, then cut that in half.

Place the fabric, finished side down, on your ironing surface and lay the freezer paper, shiny side down, on top of it. Using medium-to-high heat, press the freezer paper onto the fabric with your iron, just until bonded, being careful not to overheat it. Allow the fabric to cool and then cut it to your exact final page size.

Before printing on your fabric, trim any loose threads and be sure that its leading edge is completely bonded to the freezer paper. Re-iron the fabric if necessary to improve the bond and remove any wrinkles. Load the page into the printer so that the fabric side will be printed on.

4. Mat and frame your printed fabric with a piece of batting behind it in the area of the mat opening to "plump" the fabric up slightly as shown in Figure 2.

ABOUT THE SAMPLE (COLOR PLATE 18)

To make this piece, I first scanned an original cross-stitch pillow I completed years ago, then used photo editing software to remove the effects of age and wear. I printed the image on a Canon fabric sheet, mounted it over batting, then matted and framed it.

WHAT YOU NEED

Fusible adhesive or webbing (dry-heat type only)

Ready-to-print fabric

NOTE: *Printable iron-on fabric may be substituted for the items above and is recommended if you are using photographic images.*

1 to 1 1/3 yards of lace trim (enough to cover all edges of your printed fabric)

Fixative spray

Hot glue gun

Store-bought throw pillow, 12 x 12 inches or smaller

RECOMMENDED SOFTWARE

Creative publishing suite

Desktop publishing

Drawing

Photo editing

19. No-Sew Pillow

Add your image to a store-bought throw pillow with printed fabric mounted with iron-on adhesive.

WHAT TO DO

1. Lay out your design (see Figure 1) and size it to fit comfortably on the face of the pillow.

2. Print a proof copy of your design on plain paper and adjust it as necessary to fit your pillow.

3. Load a fabric sheet into your printer and print your design in normal mode. Allow the ink to dry overnight

4. Spray the printed fabric with fixative and allow it to dry. (For extra durability, add several more coats of spray, but note that the fabric still won't be completely waterproof or washable.)

Figure 1. A finished pillow design assembled in a drawing document.

5. Trim your printed fabric to the desired size and shape. Attach it to the pillow with fusible adhesive or webbing according to the manufacturer's instructions. (If you printed onto iron-on fabric, follow the instructions that came with it.)

6. Hot-glue lace around the printed fabric to obscure all edges and finish your pillow.

ABOUT THE SAMPLE (COLOR PLATE 19)

This pillow, made to celebrate a church anniversary, began with a scanned photograph. The border was added in a drawing program and the image was printed on iron-on fabric from Janlynn Cre8.

Printable presentation folders

20. Custom Folder

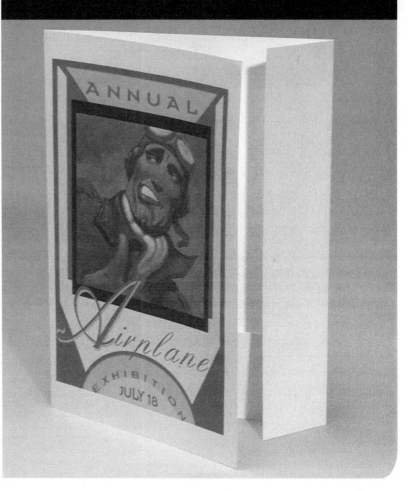

Creative publishing suite

Desktop publishing

Drawing

Lightweight folders with printable front covers and peel-and-stick assembly make for convenient custom folder production.

WHAT TO DO

1. Set a custom page size in your printer software as shown in Figure 1 (refer to your printer manual for specifics) and set the margins in your document to match the folder cover according to the dimensions given on the folder package or instructions.

1. Gift Wrap

2. Stationery

3. Photo Prints

4. Marker Board

5. Kids' Stickers

6. Do-It-Yourself Envelope

7. T-Shirt

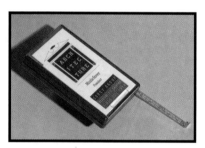

11. Tape Measure

12. Sticky Notes

13. Bookmark

8. Color Change Hidden Message

9. Game Target

10. Oversized Poster

14. Checkbook Cover

15. Traditional Greeting Cards

16. Metallic-Look Plaque

17. Holographic Business Cards

21. Notepads

22. Die-Cut Gift Tags

18. Faux Embroidery

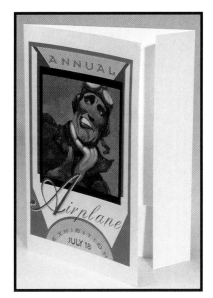

20. Custom Folder

19. No-Sew Pillow

23. White-on-Black Design

24. Custom Confetti

25. Trompe L'Oeil Apron

26. Bottle Label

27. Refrigerator Magnet

28. Candy Jar

31. Photo Calendar

32. Clock

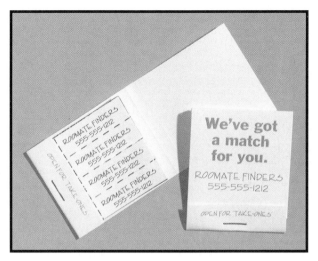

29. Matchbook Notepad

30. Cut-and-Fold Basket

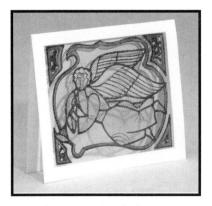

33. Antique Photo Pin

34. Imitation Stained Glass

35. Photo Standup Paper Doll

36. Round Autograph Book

37. Shaped Mouse Pad

38. Paper Tole Card

39. Shaker Card

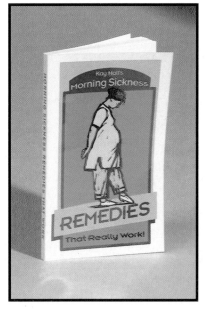

40. Paperback Book

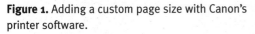

Figure 1. Adding a custom page size with Canon's printer software.

Figure 2. Cover design from Print Artist.

TIP: If your printer's software does not let you create custom page sizes, choose a larger page size than the one you need and position your design in the upper right-hand corner of the document. Then adjust your design as necessary to account for margins and so on.

2. Prepare a cover design as desired to fit within these dimensions as shown in Figure 2.

3. Print a draft copy on a piece of plain paper that is exactly the same size as the cover to check for any problems with alignment. Adjust as necessary.

4. Load the folder cover into your printer and print using the plain paper setting and the highest quality setting available (unless the folder instructions direct otherwise). Allow the ink to dry thoroughly.

5. Assemble the folder according to the package directions as shown in Figure 3.

ABOUT THE SAMPLE (COLOR PLATE 20)

This design is based on a ready-made sign layout in Print Artist 4.0. It was adjusted to print in the proper position on the oversized cover of an Essapac brand folder.

Figure 3. Assemble the cover.

WHAT YOU NEED

Chipboard (optional)

Flat work surface for binding

Hobby knife

Padding compound or thick white glue

Paintbrush or applicator for glue

Paper trimmer

Plain or colored paper

Brick or heavy book for weighing down your notepads as they dry

Wax paper

RECOMMENDED SOFTWARE

Creative publishing suite

Desktop publishing

Drawing

Chances are you use notepads every day. Now see how easy it is to make your own at home.

WHAT TO DO

1. Open a one-page document and draw a rectangle to represent the size of your notepad. (A good size is 4 x 5 inches—it can be printed four to a page with an inkjet). Add art and lettering around the edges or at the top to create a decorative, personalized border. The center section of the design should be empty (as in Figure 1) or have a simple, light-colored background, because this is where notes will be written.

2. Duplicate your note paper design on the document so that multiple copies will print on each page, as shown in Figure 1. Tile the note pad designs (butt the edges together) to minimize the number of cuts that will be required later. Remove the guide rectangles before printing and replace with crop marks if desired.

3. Print a draft copy of your design on plain paper and check for proper layout and positioning. Adjust as necessary.

4. Print the desired number of final copies on plain or colored paper using normal quality.

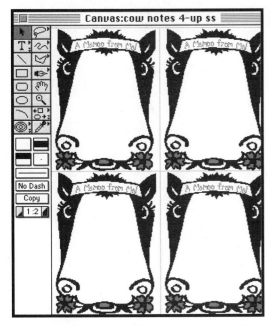

Figure 1. Multiple copies of a notepad page design laid out in a draw program.

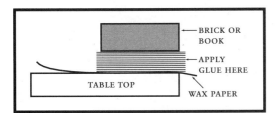

Figure 2. Notepad ready for binding.

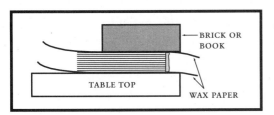

Figure 3. Glued notepad weighted down to dry.

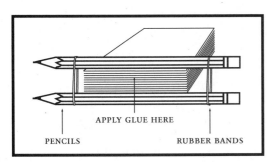

Figure 4. Clamping a very small notepad (round pencils won't work!).

5. Use a paper trimmer to separate and trim the notes to size. Stack them on a piece of chipboard cut to the same size.

6. To bind your stack, place it on a flat surface protected with wax paper (so that the glue won't get on the table and the pad won't stick to the table surface). Weight it down so the pages stay tightly stacked—cookbooks, bricks, and dictionaries are handy for this process. The page edges you want to bind should be exposed and protrude beyond the edges of your weights and work surface slightly (1/4 to 1/8 inch) as shown in Figure 2.

7. Brush the overhanging edge of the pad with a thick coat of padding compound or glue. Remove the weight, slide the pad back fully onto the table, lay a sheet of wax paper on top of the pad and weight it down again as shown in Figure 3.

   TIP: *If you're making a small pad, clamp the paper between two pencils held together by rubber bands on each end as shown in Figure 4.*

8. Allow the glue to dry thoroughly. If the padded edge doesn't seem sturdy enough, apply a second coat of glue (no clamping or weighting is needed for the second coat).

9. Once the glue is dry, trim away any excess glue with a hobby knife to finish your pad.

   TIP: *Multiple notepads can be stacked and padded at the same time. Cut them apart with a knife when dry.*

ABOUT THE SAMPLE (COLOR PLATE 21)

Our notepad design consists of text added to a border from Broderbund's ClickArt. The 50-sheet stack was "padded" with two coats of Aleene's Tacky Glue.

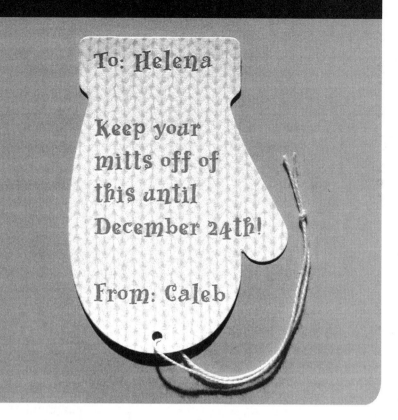

WHAT YOU NEED

Removable tape (3M Post-It Correction & Cover Up Tape preferred)

Simple die-cut paper shapes

RECOMMENDED SOFTWARE

Creative publishing suite

Desktop publishing

Drawing

Word processing

Print your design onto pre-cut paper shapes using a handy "piggyback" technique.

CAUTION: *This can be a risky project, especially with front-loading printers where the paper must make a 180° turn: the tape may come loose or an edge may catch. Please use extreme care, taking into account the idiosyncrasies of your printer.*

WHAT TO DO

1. Lay out your design on the die-cut shape, keeping in mind the shape's dimensions and the fact that you will need an unprinted margin of about 3/16 inch along the leading edges (those entering the printer first) so you can tape them down later. (See Figure 1.)

   TIP: *The larger and less complicated the die-cut shapes, the easier it will be to print on them. Hearts, balloons, and mittens are some examples of good shapes to start out with.*

2. Print a proof on plain paper in draft mode and make sure all the printing fits inside the die-cut shape with adequate room for taping. (Hold the paper and die-cut shape front of a window or other light source for better visibility.) Adjust the design as necessary.

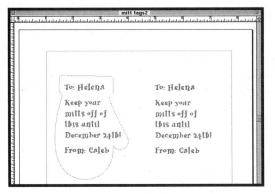

Figure 1. The scanned outline of the mitten cutout serves as a non-printing guide to help lay out the text.

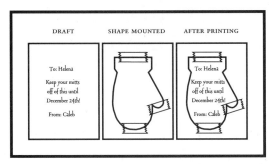

Figure 2. Design must fit onto die-cut shape.

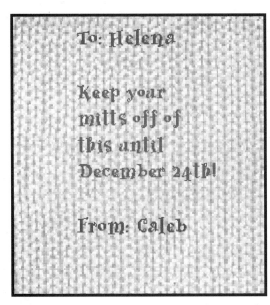

Figure 3. The sweater's knit background is large enough to cover the entire shape.

ALTERNATIVE PROCEDURE

When working with heavier die-cuts (such as light card-stock ones), you can attach the shapes to the carrier page with rubber cement instead of tape. This allows you to print over the entire surface of the shape and to include *full-bleed* designs (designs that run right to, or past, the edge of the paper). Follow the instructions on the container to bond the shape temporarily to the carrier. When the rubber cement has dried thoroughly, remove any excess with a clean finger or eraser before loading the page into the printer. After the page has printed and the ink is dry, carefully peel the shape away from the carrier and remove any remaining adhesive from the back.

3. Print a copy of the final design on plain paper in draft mode to use as a "carrier" sheet.

4. Carefully position the die-cut shape over the printed design on the carrier sheet and tape the shape in place with removable tape. This will ensure that the printing falls properly on the die-cut shape as shown in Figure 2. Make sure the die-cut shape is attached securely and that all leading or curled edges that might jam the printer are taped down.

5. Load the prepared page into your printer and print your design using the highest quality setting available.

6. When the ink is dry, carefully remove the tape, and the tag is ready to attach to a package with string or tape.

   TIP: This same procedure works nicely for printing on store-bought sticky notes (such as 3M Post-Its). If you position the note so that the adhesive edge enters the printer first, you may not need to tape the note to the "carrier" sheet.

ABOUT THE SAMPLE (COLOR PLATE 22)

A scanned sweater provides the background for these holiday gift tags (see Figure 3) printed on light card-stock shapes ready-made for rubber stamping. Rubber cement (see "Alternative Procedure" sidebar) was used instead of tape so we could print all the way to the edge on all sides.

23. White-on-Black Design

Who says you can't print on dark paper with an inkjet? It's possible with a clever technique borrowed from rubber stamping enthusiasts.

WHAT TO DO

1. Create your design in black and white (no grays). As you design, remember that the colors will be reversed (black will be white and white will be black) in the finished product (see Figure 1).

   TIP: Here are a few quick ways to visualize the final effect on your screen:

   For text designs or inline graphics (images inserted directly into a line of text as opposed to floating in a separate frame), simply drag the cursor to select the text and graphics to see the colors in reverse.

   In a photo editing program, select the image and choose the Invert command. Select Undo to go back to your original design.

   In Print Artist, select the graphic, then choose Reversed from the Color menu. Uncheck Reversed to go back to your original design.

Figure 1. An image colored properly for white on black printing, placed in a Print Artist card layout.

2. Print a draft copy on plain paper to check other design details and adjust as necessary.

3. Prepare your embossing materials (for more information on embossing, see page 36) and put a plain sheet of paper in the output tray to act as a liner and protect the printer.

4. When everything is ready, print the final copy using the printer's plain paper setting with normal print quality.

5. As soon as the printed page is ejected, cover all of the wet ink with embossing powder.

6. Remove the black paper from the printer very carefully to avoid spilling any powder.

7. Tap away excess powder and heat the powder remaining on the page according to the embossing powder's instructions.

   TIP: If the ink is drying too quickly for the powder to stick (and you're sure your printer is using pigmented ink), increase the printing speed. You'll need to experiment a bit, but a couple of suggestions are to turn off print spooling (background printing) or simplify your design so that it takes less time to print.

8. Trim and fold or mount your finished creation as desired.

ABOUT THE SAMPLE (COLOR PLATE 23)

I started with a novelty shareware font called Igloo Laser to create the design for this white-on-black card. Using a snow-capped font wasn't a great idea, though, because when the embossing technique reversed the colors, I got black "snow" on solid white letters. I finally got it fixed with some detailed editing, but it would have been easier to add black drips to outlined white letters in a paint program.

24. Custom Confetti

WHAT YOU NEED

Colored paper or coated inkjet paper

Craft punches (1/2-inch size or larger)

RECOMMENDED SOFTWARE

Creative publishing suite

Desktop publishing

Drawing

Word processing

Confetti spilling from a greeting card or announcement is a double surprise when you've custom printed it for the occasion.

WHAT TO DO

1. Measure the width and any other key dimensions of a sample cutout from your punch and type a word or initials to fit within the punch silhouette.

   TIP: *Because most printers achieve their highest resolution with black text, you'll probably get better results at these small sizes if your lettering is in black.*

2. Print a draft copy of your design to proof it and see that it fits the punch shape as expected. The easiest way to do this is to turn the punch upside down, insert the printed section of the page so that it faces you and view the design through the punch opening. Adjust the design as necessary.

3. Repeat the design (copy it) for the desired number of confetti pieces. Be sure to leave ample horizontal space between words and vertical space between lines as shown in Figure 1 to facilitate punching later.

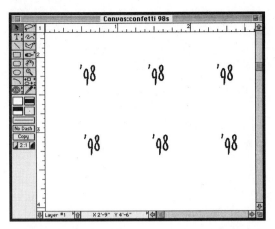

Figure 1. Confetti text layout.

Figure 2. Check for visibility and centering through punch's opening.

4. Print the final page using the highest quality setting available.

5. Cut the printed page into strips so that the punch can reach each of the words on each strip.

6. Holding the punch upside down, position the strip so that the word is completely visible and reasonably centered within the punch's opening as shown in Figure 2. Punch and repeat for each piece of confetti.

ABOUT THE SAMPLE (COLOR PLATE 24)

The initials of the school, name of the graduate, and year were printed in black on paper chosen to match school colors. A star-shaped punch turned the printouts into custom-made confetti for enclosing with graduation invitations.

Blank cotton apron (a canvas apron is okay when working with cold peel transfers)

Heat-transfer paper

Hobby knife or scissors

Household iron

Realistic photographic or scanned image(s)

25. Trompe L'Oeil Apron

RECOMMENDED SOFTWARE

Creative publishing suite

Desktop publishing

Drawing

Photo editing

Fool the eye with a garment, such as this apron, bearing transferred scans of real three-dimensional objects.

WHAT TO DO

1. Measure your apron to determine the available area for your design, paying close attention to seams and the orientation and relative positions of graphics needed. (You can not apply transfers over seams.) Create a template in your software that reflects this information.

2. Scale and position the desired design elements on your template in the proper location. These elements should be scans or photographs of actual objects—the more realistic, the better, as shown in Figure 1. It also adds to the realism if the object images will fit in your layout at actual size.

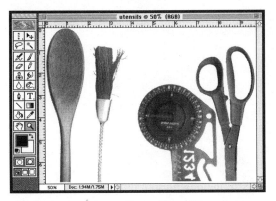

Figure 1. Scanned utensils positioned in a photo editing program.

How to Select an Item to Receive Your Transfer

- The transfer area must be flat and free of seams, bumps, or wrinkles.

- Smooth fabrics of 100% cotton or 50/50 cotton/polyester blends are ideal.

- White, neutral, or ash-colored fabrics work well. Although pastels can produce satisfactory results, the fabric's color will show through. Dark colors won't work at all.

- Fabric or fabric-covered items specifically made to be decorated (called *blanks*) will produce the best results.

- Craft stores or the craft departments of mass merchandisers like Wal-Mart offer a selection of T-shirt, vest, cap, sweatshirt, apron, tote bag, and banner blanks.

- To find more unusual items—like coasters, mouse pads, jigsaw puzzles, dolls, miniature T-shirts (for stuffed animals), Christmas stockings, neckties, or tool aprons—see the transfer supplies sources listed in Appendix C.

3. Print a draft copy of your design in mirror image on plain paper to proof and check the fit of your design on the apron.

4. Print your final copy in mirror image on transfer paper using the printer settings recommended by the paper's manufacturer.

5. Closely follow the manufacturer's instructions to trim and iron your transfer onto the apron and to peel off the transfer paper's backing.

About the Sample (Color Plate 25)

We scanned in real kitchen utensils and crafting tools (yes, right out of the drawer and onto the scanner bed) for the featured transfer on this apron. The transfer was placed just above the top of the apron pockets, so it appears that real utensils are sticking out of the pockets. Novelty fonts were used for the lettering on the top transfer and applied to the apron separately.

WHAT YOU NEED

Decorative border or corner punch

Glossy-finish acrylic spray

Metallic paper

Paper trimmer or hobby knife

Rubber cement

26. Bottle Label

RECOMMENDED SOFTWARE

Creative publishing suite

Desktop publishing

Drawing

Just about anything printed on metallic inkjet paper looks special, but it's the cleverly punched design that makes this label a real eye-catcher.

WHAT TO DO

1. Measure the target area of the bottle or jar you'd like to label (it should have a flat side or regular cylindrical shape for the label to adhere properly) and use that information to determine the size of your label.

2. Cut several rectangles of the size you determine in Step 1 from scrap paper and use them to test various punching patterns (see the examples in Figure 1) until you find one you like.

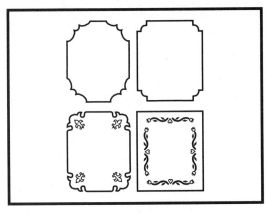

Figure 1. Choosing a punch pattern.

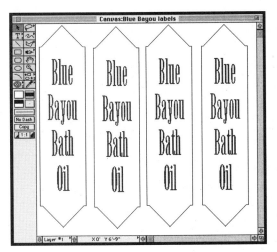

Figure 2. Multiple copies of the sample label laid out in a draw program.

3. Using the final scrap-paper model as reference, create your design to fit the label size and allow room for punching. Include crop marks or guidelines to assist in cutting out the labels. If you will be printing multiple copies of your label, duplicate the design on the page the desired number of times (see Figure 2).

4. Print a proof copy of your labels on plain paper. Cut one out and punch it as determined in Step 1 to be sure it fits the bottle and produces the desired look. Adjust the design as necessary.

5. Print the final copy of your labels on metallic paper according to the manufacturer's instructions and allow it to dry thoroughly (overnight is best).

6. Spray the page with glossy-finish acrylic spray and allow it to dry.

7. Cut out your labels and punch your design into them.

8. Attach each label to a clean bottle with rubber cement according to the instructions on the container. When the glue is dry, peel away any seepage from around the edge of the label.

NOTE: *As with any paper label, this arrangement is for light duty and will not withstand immersion in water.*

ABOUT THE SAMPLE (COLOR PLATE 26)

These labels were printed in solid blue (to match the color of the bottle) on gold metallic paper purchased from Micro Format. Because the bottle is so narrow, I didn't have room to punch all four corners of the label with a corner punch and had to improvise. My solution was to first cut the top and bottom ends of the label into a 90° point (as shown in Figure 2). Then I slipped the label ends (now shaped like a corner) into my fleur-de-lis corner lace punch from Family Treasures and punched the design you see in the photo. (This technique also works well for bookmarks.)

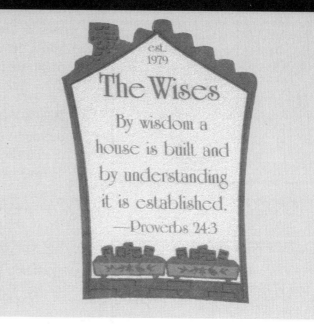

Your inkjet design, sandwiched between pressure-sensitive laminating film and adhesive-backed magnetic sheeting, becomes a great looking personalized magnet in the shape of your choice.

WHAT TO DO

1. Measure your magnet sheets to determine the maximum size for your design. Draw a temporary rectangle or place non-printing guidelines to mark the size in a new document.

2. Create a design for your magnet to fit within the size guide laid out in Step 1. For best results, choose an image with simple outlines that will be easy to cut out with scissors later.

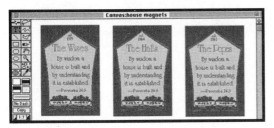

Figure 1. Multiple magnet designs composed in a draw program.

SELF-ADHESIVE LAMINATE
PRINTED PAGE
MAGNETIC SHEET

Figure 2. Layers for magnet assembly.

3. Duplicate the magnet design on the page for the desired number of copies and edit individual magnets as appropriate as shown in Figure 1.

4. Print a proof copy on plain paper to check design details and adjust as necessary.

5. Print the final copy of your magnet designs onto coated inkjet paper using the highest quality setting available and allow the ink to dry thoroughly.

6. Cover the entire printed area with clear tape or laminating film (see the layering diagram in Figure 2).

7. Separate the magnet designs from each other with scissors, leaving a margin of at least 1/16 inch all the way around each one.

8. Peel off the magnet backing and attach one of the magnet designs, making sure that none of the printed area extends past the edge of the magnet. Burnish down thoroughly.

9. Trim closely along the outline of your image with straight or decorative-edge scissors to complete the magnet.

   TIP: Cut edges of the magnet can be cleaned up by filing gently downward from the top surface with a nail file.

ABOUT THE SAMPLE (COLOR PLATE 27)

This house-shaped magnet was designed in a draw program using a ClickArt image, printed on coated inkjet paper and attached to a business card sized magnet. Both straight and decorative-edge scissors were used to trim and shape the magnet.

Batting

Container with lid made for fabric insert

Fixative spray

Ready-to-print fabric

Scissors

28. Candy Jar

Top off this candy jar, made to showcase needle-work, with your inkjet-printed fabric instead.

RECOMMENDED SOFTWARE

Creative publishing suite

Desktop publishing

Drawing

WHAT TO DO

1. Measure the key dimensions of your container's lid (including its outer edge and the inner measurement of the insert window) and create a template showing the same dimensions.

2. Design text and graphics to fit inside the lid and be visible within the viewable area of the lid as shown in Figure 1.

3. Print and trim a draft of your design on plain paper to proof and check for proper fit. Adjust the design as necessary.

Figure 1. Candy jar lid design in Print Artist.

4. Print the final copy of your design on fabric using your printer's transparency setting in normal mode and allow the ink to dry overnight.

5. Spray the printed area of the fabric with several coats of fixative, allowing the spray to dry between coats. (Remember, however, that the design will not be waterproof!)

6. When dry, cut the printed fabric to size and remove it from its carrier. (Cut a matching piece of batting, if you desire an "upholstered" look.)

7. Insert the fabric piece into the container lid (with batting underneath if desired) and secure it in place according to the manufacturer's instructions.

ABOUT THE SAMPLE (COLOR PLATE 28)

This candy jar was created with a "Country Keeper" container made by New Berlin. The design was created in Print Artist and printed on freezer paper-backed muslin.

WHAT YOU NEED

Card stock

Perforating wheel (optional)

Plain paper

Scissors, hobby knife, or paper trimmer
(preferred)

Scoring tool

Stapler

RECOMMENDED SOFTWARE

Creative publishing suite

Desktop publishing

Drawing

A simple staple and a savvy layout are the keys to
creating this nifty project, patterned after the
humble matchbook.

WHAT TO DO

1. Create a template for the matchbook-style cover according
   to the diagram in Figure 1. (The matchbook can be any size
   that will fit on a page, but we've given dimensions for a
   sample that will be 2 x 2 1/2 inches when folded closed to
   get you started.)

2. Lay out your text and graphics according to the template so
   that they will appear in the desired location on the finished
   matchbook. Duplicate the design on the page for the desired
   number of matchbooks. Leave the outer rectangles of each
   matchbook as cutting guides, but be sure to hide or remove
   fold lines so that they don't print.

3. Print a proof of your design on plain paper, cut it out, score
   along lines shown in Figure 2, and fold to assemble a sample. Check your sample for proper layout and positioning
   and adjust as necessary—be sure you have allowed enough
   space between fold lines to accommodate the thicker stock
   you'll use for your final printout. Adjust the design and layout as necessary.

Figure 1. Multiple copies of a matchbook cover
design laid out in a draw program.

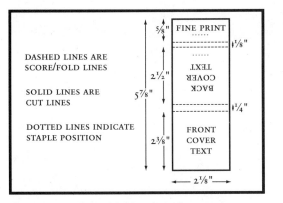

Figure 2. Cutting and folding lines for sample matchbook.

DASHED LINES ARE
SCORE/FOLD LINES

SOLID LINES ARE
CUT LINES

DOTTED LINES INDICATE
STAPLE POSITION

FINE PRINT

BACK COVER TEXT

FRONT COVER TEXT

5/8"
1/8"
2 1/2"
5 7/8"
1/4"
2 3/8"
2 1/8"

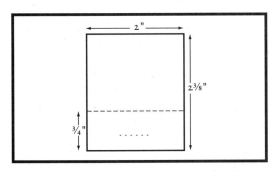

Figure 3. Perforate pages if desired to make them easier to tear out.

2"
2 3/8"
3/4"

Canvas:matchbook inserts

Figure 4. Multiple "take-one" pages laid out in a drawing program.

4. Print the final copy of your design on card stock using the highest quality setting available and allow the ink to dry.

5. Score your matchbook cover design, trim to size, and fold your matchbooks as you did your sample.

6. Cut blank paper into 2 x 2 3/8-inch sheets to make the note paper to go inside the match book. Plan on a maximum of about 6 sheets per matchbook. If desired, perforate the sheets 3/4 inch from the short side (see Figure 3) with a perforating wheel to make the pages easier to tear out. (For more information on perforating, see page 33.)

7. Using a standard matchbook as a reference if necessary, fold the lower section of the matchbook cover up, insert the note pages and staple them into the cover with a single staple. Fold the rest of the cover over the note pages and tuck it in to close and complete your matchbook.

About the Sample (Color Plate 29)

This unique item advertising a home business is made to gain attention on even the most crowded bulletin board. It was printed on glossy card stock and, instead of note paper, is filled with tearaway phone number slips as shown in Figure 4. The slips were separated from each other with scissors down to the perforation line to make it easy for a prospective customer to remove them.

WHAT YOU NEED

Card stock

Embellishments (optional)

Fixative spray (optional)

Glue stick

Scissors or hobby knife

30. Cut-and-Fold Basket

Make cute table decorations to match the theme of your party using card stock printed with a cut-and-fold design.

WHAT TO DO

1. Open a ready-made gift basket template (see Figure 1) or design your own template using Figure 2 for reference.

2. Add text and graphics to the layout or edit as desired.

3. Print a draft copy of your design on plain paper. Cut along all the outer lines and fold it into a mockup basket. Check the mockup for design details and adjust your layout as necessary.

4. Print the final copy on card stock using the highest quality setting available and allow the ink to dry thoroughly.

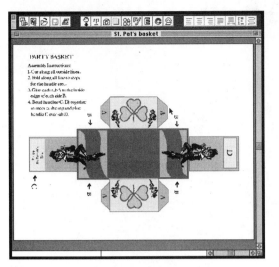

Figure 1. A ready-made basket design from Print Artist.

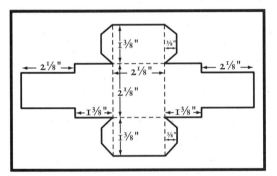

Figure 2. Template for designing your own gift basket.

5. Spray the final copy with fixative if you plan to add embellishments, such as glitter glue, to help prevent the liquid glue from damaging printed areas.

6. Cut out the basket with scissors or a hobby knife. For neater folds, score along the fold lines (see page 33 for information about scoring).

7. Outline or highlight key areas of the design with glitter glue as desired and allow to dry overnight.

8. Fold the tabs down (toward the unprinted side), then fold the four basket sides into position.

9. Using glue, attach each tab inside the adjacent basket wall and connect the handle halves together at the top. (Paper clips will help hold the basket together until the glue dries.)

ABOUT THE SAMPLE (COLOR PLATE 30)

This St. Patrick's Day basket is one of the ready-made projects in Print Artist 4.0. It was printed on Beckett Enhance stock, then embellished with glitter glue before assembly. Filling the basket with chocolate coins would complete the "pot of gold" motif.

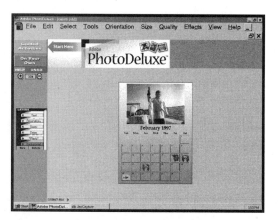

Figure 1. A calendar page designed in Adobe PhotoDeluxe using the Guided Activities feature.

31. Photo Calendar

Smart software makes calendar printing convenient, and a simple ribbon binding ties the project together for twelve months of smiles.

WHAT TO DO

1. Select twelve photographs for your calendar and scan them if they are not already in digital form. Edit them as desired in your photo editing software, cropping them, correcting color, and so on. Scale each photo to approximately 4 x 6 inches or other dimension specified by your calendar software.

2. Prepare the monthly calendar pages as shown in Figure 1 according to your software's instructions. This might include opening a calendar template, opening a new calendar document or following a procedure on screen.

3. Import photos and insert text and/or graphics for holidays, family birthdays, and other important events on your calendar pages as desired.

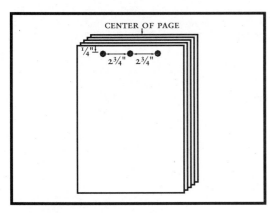

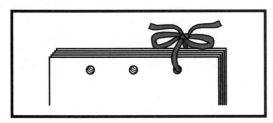

Figure 2. Punch holes for ribbon.

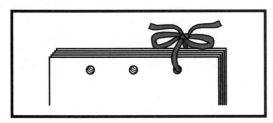

Figure 3. Tying the knot.

4. Print a draft copy of each calendar page in grayscale on plain paper to proof. Check for centering and adjust your design as necessary.

5. Print the final copy of each month's calendar on coated paper using the highest quality setting available.

6. Design a front cover for your calendar. A simple title, such as "Hall Family 1998" centered on the page, will usually work well.

7. Print a draft copy of your cover on plain paper to proofread and check for centering. Adjust your design as necessary.

8. Print the final copy of your cover on card stock using the highest quality setting available. You can use a blank piece of the same card stock for the back cover.

9. Mark the locations for hole punching with a pencil at the top of the sheet of card stock you'll be using as the back cover. First mark the center with a 1/4-inch line 1/4 inch from the edge, then make two more pencil lines 2 3/4 inches away from the center line on either side.

10. Punch holes in the back cover at the pencil lines as shown in Figure 2.

11. Use the back cover as a punching template to punch holes in all calendar pages and the front cover so that all the holes will line up when the completed calendar is stacked for binding.

12. Apply hole reinforcements around each hole on the back side of each page and cover.

13. Cut ribbon in half. Thread one piece of ribbon through the right-hand hole and tie the ends together so that there is enough slack that the pages can easily be flipped. Secure the knot and tie a bow on top of it as shown in Figure 3. With another section of ribbon, tie a matching knot and bow through the left-hand hole. Leave the center hole open to allow hanging the calendar on a hook or a nail.

ABOUT THE SAMPLE (COLOR PLATE 31)

I simply followed Adobe PhotoDeluxe through a "Guided Activity" to create each month's calendar page. Small graphics included as "decorations" in PhotoDeluxe mark special days on the calendar, which was printed on heavyweight coated inkjet paper with card-stock covers.

WHAT YOU NEED

Card stock

Circle cutter

Double-sided tape or glue

Nail scissors or hobby knife

Protective coating spray

Wall clock or clock kit

RECOMMENDED SOFTWARE

Creative publishing suite

Desktop publishing

Drawing

Customize a store-bought clock with a new face you print yourself and get great results every time.

WHAT TO DO

1. If your clock is already assembled, carefully pry off its crystal with a screwdriver, remove the hands, and store them in a safe location.

2. Remove the existing clock face and measure its diameter.

3. Open a clock template in your software and resize it as required, or design your own template to fit your clock, as shown in Figure 1.

    TIP: If you have a clip art image of a clock (head-on view), import it to use as a layout guide rather than starting from scratch.

4. Print a draft of your design in grayscale on plain paper to proof and check for fit against the clock face you removed in Step 2.

Figure 1. A clock face design laid out in a drawing program.

5. Print the final copy of your design on card stock using the highest quality setting available. Allow the ink to dry thoroughly.

6. Spray your printout with protective coating spray (preferably UV rated to protect colors) and allow the coating to dry.

7. Cut out the clock face with a circle cutter set to the appropriate diameter. With fingernail scissors or a hobby knife, make a hole in the center just large enough to accommodate the center post.

8. Place the new clock face over the clock's center post and rotate it into true position. Secure it in place with glue or double-sided adhesive tape.

9. Carefully reinstall the clock's hands at the 12:00 position to ensure proper calibration.

10. Replace the clock's crystal, install the battery (or plug in to an outlet), and set the time according to the manufacturer's instructions.

ABOUT THE SAMPLE (COLOR PLATE 32)

The dinosaur clock face was adapted from a timepiece graphic exported from Print Shop. The inexpensive 8-inch Ingraham clock was easily taken apart, modified, and reassembled.

WHAT YOU NEED

Clear nail polish

Craft glue

Embellishments (fabric scraps, lace, ribbon, beads, charms, etc.)

Inkjet-compatible shrink plastic sheet

Photo in digital form (see note below about selection)

Store-bought pin back

RECOMMENDED SOFTWARE

Creative publishing suite

Desktop publishing

Drawing

Photo editing

Turn a vintage photograph into a lovely piece of Victorian-themed jewelry by first printing it onto inkjet shrink plastic.

WHAT TO DO

1. Select or scan a photo for use as your pin's central image. Its printed size should be two to three times the desired finished size, but it needn't be high resolution (see Figure 1). (When we shrink it, its resolution will double or triple.) Refer to shrink plastic package directions for specifics.

   NOTE: *Shrink plastic behaves somewhat unpredictably during the heating phase. Choose photos or graphics that will be "distortion tolerant." For instance, straight lines and contemporary photos of recognizable people should be avoided because lines may bend and proportions may change as the images shrink down.*

Figure 1. Image should be two to three times larger than the final jewelry size.

2. Load a shrink plastic sheet into your printer and print your photo on it according to the shrink plastic package directions.

3. Allow your print to dry thoroughly (overnight is best).

4. When dry, shrink the image according to package directions and allow the shrunken piece to cool completely.

5. Coat the printed side of the shrunken piece with clear nail polish and allow it to dry thoroughly.

   TIP: *To make the shrunken piece more opaque, coat the back side with white nail polish or correction fluid.*

6. Embellish your completed pin as desired and glue a pin back onto it.

ABOUT THE SAMPLE (COLOR PLATE 33)

This sample, featuring an antique family photo, was provided by Micro Format, makers of an inkjet-compatible shrink plastic. A crocheted doily, treated with fabric stiffener, and charms were used as embellishments.

34. Imitation Stained Glass

Selective embossing, accomplished with multiple printing passes, is the secret to creating the stained-glass look, complete with metallic "leading." The image is great for mounting in a greeting card or suncatcher when you're done.

WHAT TO DO

1. Find or create a graphic suitable for a stained glass window—one that has clean edges and bold lines, so it can be separated into color and black outline versions. (The image in Figure 1 is a good example of a suitable graphic.)

2. Remove (or change to white) the black outlines that represent the leading in the stained glass to leave only the color panes as shown in Figure 2. Save this file or layer as "color."

3. Next, go back to the original image and delete (or change to white) the parts of the image that represent the glass to produce the black "outline" version as shown in Figure 3. Save this file or layer as "outline." Be careful not to shift the image at all, because it must print in exactly the same location on the page as the color file.

Figure 1. The stained glass graphic before separation.

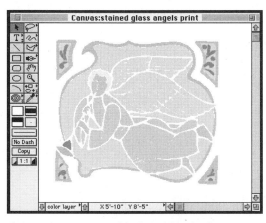

Figure 2. Image minus black outlines for first pass.

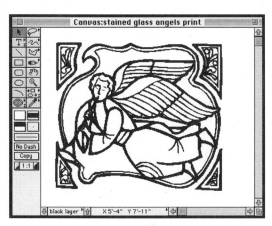

Figure 3. Outlines only for second pass.

4. Load plain paper into your printer and print the "color" file. To avoid problems with alignment between passes, be sure to load the paper carefully into your printer each time—flush against the fixed guide and against the printer's intake. When the ink is dry, reload the printed paper into your printer (head first) and print the "outline" version on top of the "color" version. Use the resulting composite image to proof your stained glass creation and adjust design, layout, and orientation as necessary. When the two images are printed as a composite, they should look like one image with no new overlaps or gaps.

5. After making any necessary adjustments to your files and proofing again if necessary, load transparency film into your printer for final printing. Again, be sure you load the film flush with the fixed guide and the intake on every pass. Print the "color" version on the film first using your printer's transparency setting and the highest print quality available. Allow the ink to dry overnight.

   TIP: To produce more intense colors on transparency film, allow the ink to dry from the first pass and then print the color version a second time, directly over the first pass.

6. Prepare your embossing area and materials (for more information see page 36). When everything is ready, reload the printed transparency film into your printer (head first) and print the black "outline" version over the "color" printout using your printer's normal setting. See Figure 3.

7. As soon as the page is ejected from the printer, move the printed film from the output tray to your embossing area. (When printing on film, as opposed to paper, you have time to remove the printout from the printer before dumping on the powder.)

8. Immediately cover all wet ink with embossing powder. Tap away excess and heat the film according to the instructions that came with the powder. Do not overheat, or film will warp!

9. Trim and mount your stained glass as desired.

ABOUT THE SAMPLE (COLOR PLATE 34)

The angel stained glass design, from Broderbund's ClickArt, was prepared using a drawing program and its layering features to overlay the color and outline versions (rather than creating two separate documents as described above). Antique silver embossing powder was used over the black outlines.

WHAT YOU NEED

Clean foam meat trays (from the grocery store)

Full-sheet inkjet label stock with permanent adhesive

Glue stick with removable adhesive

Hobby knife

Plain or coated paper

RECOMMENDED SOFTWARE

Creative publishing suite

Desktop publishing

Drawing

Photo editing

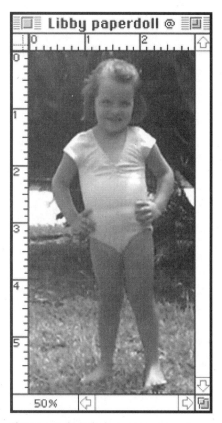

Figure 1. A digital photo cropped and resized to fit the foam sheet.

Here's a fresh take on an old pastime—what child won't love paper dolls featuring a picture of herself?

WHAT TO DO

1. Cut the vertical sides from the foam tray and measure the length of the remaining flat foam sheet.

2. Choose a photograph to be used as the doll, scan it, and import it into your photo editing program. (If the photo is already in digital form, simply open it.) Crop and resize the imported photo to fit on the foam sheet, up to a maximum of about 7 inches tall (see Figure 1).

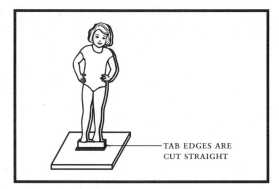

Figure 2. Leave a tab at the foot of the doll.

TAB EDGES ARE
CUT STRAIGHT

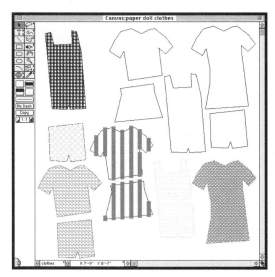

Figure 3. Paper doll clothes designed, duplicated, and filled in with patterns in a drawing program.

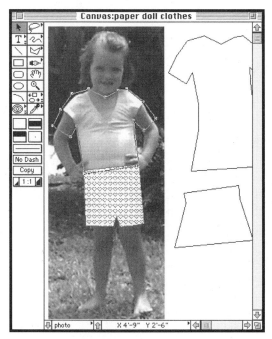

Figure 4. Using the digital photo on screen as a guide for designing clothes.

3. Print a draft copy of your photo on plain paper to proof it. Check its size, color, contrast, and so on and adjust your image as necessary.

4. Load label stock into your printer and print your photo on it using the highest quality setting available.

5. Cut the image out of the label stock, leaving about 1/4-inch margin all the way around, then peel off the label backing and attach the image to the foam.

6. Using a hobby knife, trim along the outline of your mounted doll, leaving a foam tab at least 1/4-inch high by 1 inch wide at its feet as shown in Figure 2.

7. Shape a section of the remaining foam into a base. Cut a slot in it to receive the foam tab at the doll's feet (it should be a tight fit) and trim off any foam that protrudes below the base so that the doll can stand up.

8. Draw outlines of clothing pieces in a draw or paint program as shown in Figure 3. Fill the clothes with textile or patterned backgrounds, or you can leave only the outlines for children to color in.

9. Print a draft copy of the clothing pieces on plain paper, cut them out, and check to see that they fit the doll. Adjust as necessary.

10. Print final copies on plain or coated inkjet paper.

11. Cut out the clothing pieces and apply a stripe of removable adhesive with a glue stick to the back of each. Let the adhesive dry per manufacturer's instructions and store ready-to-use pieces on a clean sheet of paper.

ABOUT THE SAMPLE (COLOR PLATE 35)

The doll was made from a photo taken with a digital camera. A low-resolution version of the image was imported into a draw program and used in the background layer as a guide for outlining the clothes (as shown in Figure 4).

Access to plastic comb-binding equipment

Archival quality paper

Binding comb (size according to number of pages desired)

Card stock

Circle cutter

Clean sheet of stiff cardboard at least 6 x 6 inches (thin enough to be cut with a circle cutter)

Paper trimmer

Self-adhesive laminating sheets or self-adhesive clear cover

RECOMMENDED SOFTWARE

Desktop publishing

Drawing

Comb-binding is known for being neat and inexpensive, but pre-shaped pages can make comb-bound documents fun as well.

WHAT TO DO

1. Create a new document in your software and draw a 6-inch circle on the page. Add a horizontal line 7/8 inch below the top of the circle as shown in Figure 1. The area inside the circle below the line represents the size and shape of the autograph book.

2. Design the front cover of your autograph book using the circle and line as size guides as shown in Figure 2. (You'll ultimately remove and discard the area above the line to produce an edge for binding.) When your design is complete, remove or hide the guide circle and horizontal line if necessary so that they will not print on your final cover.

3. Print a draft copy of your cover design on plain paper and correct dimensions or other design details.

4. Print the final copy of your cover on card stock using the highest quality setting available. Allow the ink to dry.

5. Laminate your cover with self-adhesive film, cut it out with a circle cutter set for a diameter of exactly 6 inches, and set it aside.

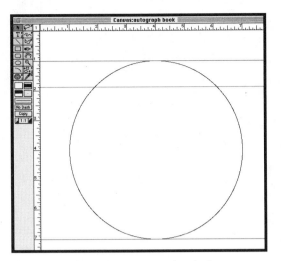

Figure 1. Setting up a cover template in Canvas.

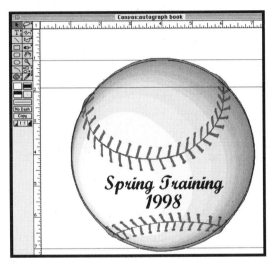

Figure 2. Designing the cover in Canvas.

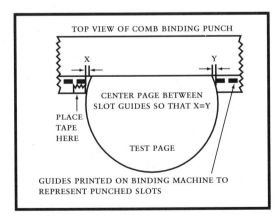

Figure 3. Position sample pages to punch binding comb slots.

6. Without readjusting the circle cutter, cut one 6-inch circle from archival quality paper (so the autographs will last for decades, provided they are written with permanent ink) for each page in your autograph book, plus several extras from scrap paper. Cut another 6-inch circle from stiff cardboard to serve as your back cover.

7. Stack the front and back covers and trim off the top 7/8 inch (measured exactly) with a paper cutter. Stack as many interior page circles as can be cut comfortably at one time with your paper trimmer and trim off exactly 7/8 inch from them also. Repeat for as many stacks as necessary until all circles are trimmed.

TIP: Mark the 5 1/8-inch (6 inches minus 7/8 inch) point on the paper trimmer with a piece of low-tack tape (like masking tape) to use as a guide for consistent cutting.

8. To determine the correct position for punching the binding comb slots, insert one of the extra scrap-paper cut circles in the comb-binding punch until the flat edge is flush against the backstop (just as you would for normal rectangular pages). Ignore the left-hand stop and instead slide the pages as shown in Figure 3 so that the visible part of the circle is centered between two of the guide rectangles (that represent the punching slots) as shown. Use low-tack tape or a pencil to mark a reference point on the punch platform for consistent punching, then line the sample up with the tape and punch. Remove the sample and verify that the slots are correctly positioned along the flat edge of the circle. If not, adjust the tape and punch another sample to check.

9. Using the tape as a guide, punch the covers and interior pages (as many at a time as the punch can comfortably handle) as you did the final sample in Step 8 until all the pages are punched.

10. Stack the covers with the blank pages in between so that the edges and binding slots line up. Insert the plastic comb using the comb-binding machine according to the manufacturer's instructions. Snip off any excess binding strip with scissors to finish.

ABOUT THE SAMPLE (COLOR PLATE 36)

The cover for our spring training autograph book was designed in Canvas using a baseball clip art image from Corel Print House and printed on Geo Card smooth card stock. It includes 15 pages—enough for dozens of autographs.

37. Shaped Mouse Pad

WHAT YOU NEED

3 mm-thick craft foam sheet (9 x 12-inch sheet)

Double-sided adhesive sheets (enough to cover the surface area of your mouse pad, preferably in no more than 2 or 3 sections)

Inkjet-coated satin-finish fabric

NOTE: *The mouse pad kit from Rayven may be substituted for the above three items.*

Coated paper

Glossy-finish acrylic spray

Scissors or hobby knife

RECOMMENDED SOFTWARE

Creative publishing suite

Desktop publishing

Drawing

Photo editing

An image printed on inkjet-coated satin-finish fabric tops this mouse pad made of layered craft materials.

WHAT TO DO

1. Select or create a design for your mouse pad to fit on an 8 1/2 x 11-inch page. Choose a design with a clean outer edge that can be easily cut (see Figure 1). Minimum size for a functional mouse pad is about 8 x 7 inches.

2. Print a proof copy of your design on coated paper using the normal setting. Check your image for size, color, contrast, and so on and adjust it as required, but note that colors will look different, usually darker, when printed on the satin-finish fabric.

Figure 1. Mouse pad design in Adobe PhotoDeluxe.

PRINTED PAGE

DOUBLE-SIDED
ADHESIVE

CRAFT FOAM

Figure 2. Layering for mouse pad assembly.

3. Print the final copy of your design on satin fabric according to the manufacturer's instructions. Allow the ink to dry thoroughly, preferably overnight.

4. Spray your printout with the glossy acrylic and let it dry.

5. Peel away the backing from one side of the double-sided adhesive and apply it to the back side of your printed fabric so that the entire design area is covered all the way to, or extending past, the edges. (You should be able to easily see the ink from the back side to help you position the adhesive.) The adhesive sheets can be applied in several sections, but align the edges side by side rather than overlapping them to avoid a bumpy mouse pad.

6. Cut the design out of the printed fabric sheet (now backed with the adhesive sheets) leaving at least an 1/8-inch margin all the way around to allow for final trimming.

7. Remove the second side of the backing from the adhesive and apply your printed design carefully to the craft foam sheet, making sure that all of the printed area is backed by the foam. See Figure 2 for layering diagram.

8. To finish, cut around the outside of the design with scissors or hobby knife to trim your mouse pad to its final shape. (If necessary, clean scissors with nail polish remover.)

ABOUT THE SAMPLE (COLOR PLATE 37)

We merged a baby photo with a stock photograph in a photo editing program to create the design for this flower-shaped mouse pad. The original photos are shown on page 13. Therm O Web Peel N'Stick was used to attach the printed fabric to a Darice Foamies sheet.

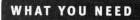

WHAT YOU NEED

Card stock

Double-sided foam tape or mounting dots

Scissors or hobby knife

38. Paper Tole Card

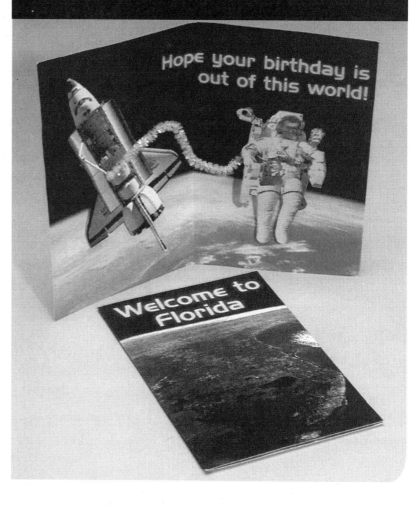

RECOMMENDED SOFTWARE

Creative publishing suite

Desktop publishing

Drawing

Greeting card

Adhesive foam dots lift key parts of your image off the page to create a dynamic-looking three-dimensional card.

WHAT TO DO

1. Create an original card design as shown (see Figure 1) or modify an existing one to be used as the basis of your paper tole card. Your design should include elements that you want to raise off the surface of your finished card, just as the Space Shuttle does in our sample project.

2. Print a proof of your basic flat card design on plain paper so you can check and correct any design or layout problems. Be sure to fold your proof as you would your finished card to be sure that planned raised elements will not interfere with the fold.

Figure 1. The base image for the card.

HOW TO CREATE A SOFT DROP SHADOW

Increasingly, photo editing software programs include an automatic command to create drop shadows, but if yours doesn't, here's how to do it yourself. First copy the image to be shadowed to a separate document or layer. Next, select the copied image, fill it with black, deselect it, and apply the Blur command. Finally, place this blurred copy of the object's silhouette behind it and slightly offset to one side and/or below your original image (judge the distance by eye on screen) to produce a soft drop shadow.

3. Print the final copy of your base card on card stock using the highest quality setting available and set it aside.

4. On card stock print out the elements you plan to raise off the page. (This could be just a second printout of your base card or a separate page with additional elements, depending on your design.) Allow the ink to dry thoroughly.

5. Cut the tole elements out of the second printed copy and set them aside.

6. Trim, score, and fold your card base as desired.

7. Mount the cutout elements from Step 5 on foam dots and apply them to the card wherever you want them to appear (usually directly on top of the base copy). Repeat this procedure to build additional layers on top of the cutouts if desired.

ABOUT THE SAMPLE (COLOR PLATE 38)

This Space Shuttle card was composed in a photo editing program using public domain images downloaded from NASA Web sites. The glow around the letters was created using the drop-shadow technique (see sidebar above), but using yellow instead of black for the shadow color. As an afterthought, an astronaut was dangled from the shuttle bay with a sparkly chenille stem (pipe cleaner).

BEST WISHES, MISS FIELD

We'll Miss You!

No one can resist these fascinating three-dimensional cards with tiny little surprises rattling around inside.

WHAT TO DO

1. Before beginning, sketch out your idea for a shaker card including a background layer that will be visible through the shaker card window and a foreground layer that will "frame" that window. The foreground and the background will be separated by a spacer layer, which also serves to trap small objects inside the card as shown in Figure 1.

   TIP: If you aren't familiar with shaker cards, visit a rubber stamping store or thumb through some rubber stamping books or magazines for great ideas and inspiration.

2. To begin designing the layers for your card, first draw a rectangle to represent the outer dimensions of your card.

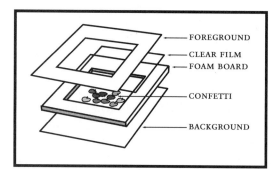

FOREGROUND

CLEAR FILM

FOAM BOARD

CONFETTI

BACKGROUND

Figure 1. Anatomy of a shaker card.

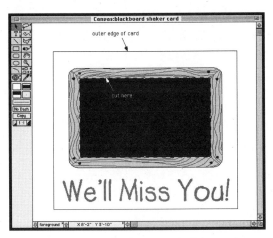

Figure 2. Design for the foreground of the card.

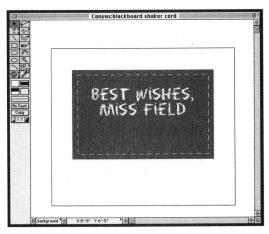

Figure 3. Designing the background using the foreground's cut line as a guide.

Figure 4. The design for the background layer of the card, ready to print.

TIP: If you're designing the card to fit a certain envelope size, make it smaller than the envelope by about 1/2 inch in both length and width to accommodate the extra thickness of the finished card.

3. Select the foreground graphic you'd like to "frame" the shaker-card window. Typical graphics would be a fishbowl, a crystal ball, or a seed packet. In our example we used a wooden blackboard frame. Place the chosen graphic within the rectangle you drew in Step 2 and draw a rectangle or circle inside the foreground graphic to represent the outer edge (and cut line) for the card window (the inner edge of the blackboard frame in our example). Be sure there is at least a 3/4-inch margin between the cut line and the outer edge of the card on all sides. Add any additional text or graphics to the foreground (outside the cutting line) and save this file as "foreground." (See Figure 2.)

4. Remove everything but the outer rectangle and the inner cut line from the "foreground" file. Inside the cut line, add the text and graphics you'd like to appear on the background of your card (behind the clear window and shakables). Extend color or texture in the background 1/8 inch outside the cutting line all the way around as shown in Figure 3, so unprinted white space doesn't show inside the frame in the finished card.

5. When you've finished designing the background, remove the cutting line as shown in Figure 4 and save this file as "background."

6. Print a draft copy of each layer and cut out the pieces to create a rough mockup so you can proof your design. Adjust the design for one or both layers as necessary so that your card will assemble properly and look the way you want it to. (Save the final correct foreground layer draft for Step 8.)

7. Print the final copies of the foreground and background on card stock using the highest quality setting available.

8. Trim both layers to size and cut out the window opening from the foreground layer just outside the cut line. Using the draft copy of the foreground layer as a layout guide, cut a piece of foam board to use as the spacer between the layers.

TIP: Cut the opening in the foam about 1/4 larger than the opening on the foreground so that rough edges of the foam won't show through the window of the assembled card.

9. Cut a piece of transparent film about an inch larger than the cutout window in length and width. Center it on the back side of the foreground layer's opening and attach it with adhesive tape or glue.

TIP: For a more complex design, print additional images on inkjet-compatible transparency film and use that for the window.

10. Tape or glue the foam board spacer to the back side of the foreground layer and transparent sheet. Lay the assembled foreground layer, window, and foam face down to insert the "shakables," then attach the background layer to seal the shakables inside the card.

TIP: Static electricity can cause confetti or other lightweight shakables to stick to the clear window. To prevent this, gently wipe the inside of the window with a used fabric softener sheet before attaching the background.

ABOUT THE SAMPLE (COLOR PLATE 39)

In this farewell card to a teacher, a shaker card became the means for adding interest to the tired old blackboard-and-apples motif. Beckett Enhance paper was used for both layers, and wood veneer tape was ironed onto the foreground layer before final assembly. Double-sided foam mounting tape, instead of foam board, adds the depth between the layers. We filled the card with confetti we made from plain red paper using an apple-shaped craft punch. One great idea would be to print each classmate's name on an apple using the technique from the Custom Confetti project (page 90) before inserting the apples in the card.

WHAT YOU NEED

Access to a heavy-duty commercial paper cutter (through a local printer or copy shop)

Frying pan or electric skillet with a flat bottom area large enough to accommodate the spine of your book

Hot glue gun and glue sticks

Lightweight card stock (65- to 80-pound cover)

Paper trimmer

Release paper (leftover backing from self-stick labels, for example)

Removable tape

Scoring tool

Self-adhesive laminating sheet (optional)

Text-weight paper

RECOMMENDED SOFTWARE

FOR COVER:

Creative publishing suite

Desktop publishing

Drawing

FOR PAGES:

Desktop publishing

Word processing plus booklet printing

If you've got a book worth binding, here's a technique that'll make it look like a store-bought paperback.

WHAT TO DO

1. Design, print, and trim your book pages so that they are 8 1/2 x 5 1/2 inches with 3/4-inch margins all around (see "How to Prepare the Interior Pages of Your Book" sidebar). Sort and stack the pages of your book as they will appear in the finished product as shown in Figure 1. Alternately, cut the desired number of plain paper sheets in half to make a blank book.

2. Measure the height of the stack of pages to determine the width of the spine that will be needed on the book's cover. Pinch the stack together firmly at the edge you are measuring to get an accurate reading.

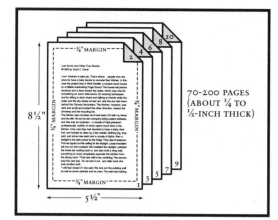

Figure 1. Book pages sorted, trimmed, and ready to bind.

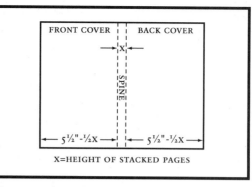

Figure 2. Layout of entire cover: front, back, and spine.

Figure 3. Cover design in Print Artist.

Figure 4. Mask edges of spine on inside surface of your cover.

3. Design a cover to wrap around the pages, taking the spine width into consideration as shown in Figures 2 and 3.

4. Print a draft copy of the cover in grayscale on a piece of card stock that is the same weight you will be using for your final cover. Score a fold line on both sides of the spine as shown in Figure 2 and fold the cover. Insert the stack of pages to verify fit and see how the cover looks (don't worry about pages sticking out, because they will be trimmed later). Adjust your cover design as necessary.

5. Print the final copy of your cover on card stock using the highest quality setting available and, if desired, laminate the printed side only using a self-adhesive laminating sheet.

6. Score the inside of the final cover at both edges of the spine as you did in Step 4.

7. Mask off the area between the scores with removable tape so that the inside of the spine is exposed as shown in Figure 4.

8. With a hot glue gun, lay down lines of glue like rungs on a ladder (1/2 to 3/8 inch apart) along the length of the inside surface of the spine, starting and ending about 1/4 inch from the top and bottom of the cover as shown in Figure 4.

9. Allow the glue to cool completely until it is solid.

10. With a knife, carefully cut the glue lines only (do not cut the cover!) along each score.

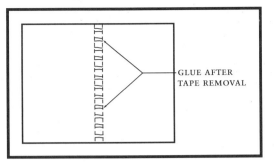

Figure 5. Glue remains on inside surface of spine after masking tape is removed.

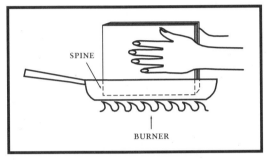

Figure 6. Stand the book on its spine in the skillet; support the covers to keep book upright.

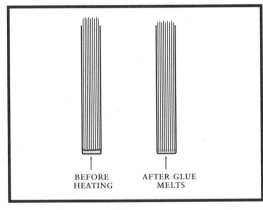

Figure 7. The pages will drop down into the glue as the glue melts.

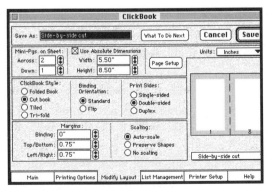

Figure 8. Layout settings in ClickBook.

11. Carefully remove the tape from along the edges of the spine, leaving the glue bands on the inside of the cover's spine only as shown in Figure 5.

12. Fold the cover at the scores and insert the stack of pages as evenly as possible.

13. Preheat your skillet or electric frying pan to medium heat (about 350° F) and place a sheet of label backing in the pan, shiny side up, to protect the cover.

14. Place the book into the skillet spine down, so the spine rests flat on the bottom of the skillet. Support the front and back covers loosely between your hands to keep the book upright as shown in Figure 6.

15. As the glue melts, the pages sink into it. Remove the book from the heat after about 30 seconds or when you can see from both ends that the pages have dropped down into the glue and are resting against the inside of the spine as shown in Figure 7. Allow the glue to cool completely.

16. Have the edges trimmed on a commercial cutting machine at a local print or copy shop.

    TIP: *You will typically be billed for this service by the number of cuts, so have several books stacked and cut at once to save money.*

ABOUT THE SAMPLE (COLOR PLATE 40)

I designed the cover for this blank book in Print Artist, then printed it on Geo Card smooth card stock. I laminated it with a self-adhesive laminating sheet, which added a nice gloss finish as well as protection. The binding was done in a frying pan on the stove, and Kinko's copy shop did the final trimming for $1 per cut.

How to Prepare the Interior Pages of Your Book

Preparing cut book pages with an inkjet printer is a complicated desktop publishing challenge that I do not recommend without the assistance of ClickBook, an inexpensive booklet printing utility from Blue Squirrel Software (see Appendix C for contact info). Follow the instructions in ClickBook to set up your book in a word processing or desktop publishing program, then use it to print in cut-book format using the layout settings shown in Figure 8 (you may choose different scaling options).

Cut the printed pages in half with a paper trimmer to separate the book pages and stack them in sequential order according to the finishing instructions in ClickBook.

I've gathered valuable information into the following sections to make it easy for you to prepare the projects listed in this book, as well as the ideas you'll inevitably come up with on your own. You'll find listings for traditional craft supplies as well as contact information for the latest in materials and techniques. I've also listed books, Web sites, and other sources of some exciting ideas. There is no end to the possibilities when you put your creative spirit to work!

3

Part 3 Resources

Selling What You Make

Sooner or later someone will see one of your computer creations and ask if they can pay you to make one for them. Or maybe you're thinking that customized crafts like the ones shown in this book could be the basis for the home business you've dreamed about. Either way, here are a few things to think about before—and after—you take the plunge.

THE RIGHT PRICE

If you're thinking of selling the products you make, pricing is the first thing to consider. Can the items you make actually bring in a profit? To find out, first determine the maximum and minimum prices feasible.

The maximum is simply the highest price the market will bear: What is the most a customer will pay for a product? Check at retailers to see what similar store-bought items cost. Check with catalogs or craftspeople to see what they sell their products for. Ask friends who'll give you an honest answer.

To determine the lowest price that makes sense, you have to determine what an item costs you to make. Add up the costs of all the craft materials and media that go into a project, and also consider the following:

- INK FOR YOUR PRINTER. This can be difficult to estimate: A standard page of black text uses just a few cents' worth of ink, but a full-page photo can easily eat up a dollar's worth, not counting special paper. For a typical (one-sided) craft page, $0.40 to $0.50 would be a good starting guess for ink. Keep a log of everything you print and how often you have to replace cartridges over the course of a few months to refine your estimates.

- EQUIPMENT DEPRECIATION. This equals at least a few cents a page, based on the fact that each project brings your printer and computer a little closer to needing replacement.

- YOUR LABOR. Decide on a figure you feel is fair—some projects need more expertise and design sense; others less.

- Custom Orders. For custom items, don't forget to factor in design time and ink cost for trial runs. (This can be quite significant, so it's a good idea to ask for a deposit up front on custom work.) The entire cost of any special materials you have to order should be covered by the customer, unless you're sure you'll use them for other clients within a reasonable amount of time. The more you can draw on designs and materials you already have on hand, the better off you will be. It keep your costs down, and customers will also be able to decide more easily if you present them with fewer choices.

Add all this up to arrive at your actual cost. The product should be priced at two to three times that amount as a rule of thumb if you want the business to be profitable. If that minimum price is more than the market will bear, you'll have to try something else. Consider different products or a different market, perhaps a particular niche of more specialized items.

MAKING IT OFFICIAL

If you've made it past the sometimes-discouraging price calculations and decide you're ready to go for it, it's time to establish yourself as a legal business. If you plan to work out of your home, check first to see what special provisions your city or neighborhood may have.

You will almost certainly need to select and register a business name before you begin filling out other applications. Give this some serious thought, with your long-term goals in mind. For instance, a business called "Kay's Krafty Kreations" might lack credibility with business clients. On the other hand, the local craft mall might be hesitant to deal with "Hall International Enterprises."

Local and state requirements to set up a business vary widely, but typically you'll need a fictitious name certificate, one or more business licenses, and a tax ID number. Yes, you will probably be required to collect sales tax on products you sell, but on the positive side you'll be able to buy your raw materials tax-free. Be sure to check on all state and local restrictions that might apply to your business, especially if you plan to work from your home.

Once you have set up a business, you will be able to deduct the cost of materials, supplies, some equipment, and other costs associated with doing business from your income at tax time. Consult with a local tax specialist to find out what's deductible and what's

not. Also remember that, as your business grows, you will need to add increasing overhead costs (office space, advertising, administrative help, bookkeeping, and so on) back in to the cost of your products.

MARKETING IDEAS

Word-of-mouth advertising is a powerful tool in this kind of business. Don't be shy; let everyone know what you're up to. Once you're up and running, or maybe even before then, it's not uncommon to receive calls from friends and friends of friends. Take advantage of this and reciprocate whenever you can—that's right, network.

Although you're certainly free to choose traditional advertising (such as in the local newspaper) or use the World Wide Web, it's most effective to let your products do the talking. For instance, make your business card a craft of some kind so that your creative talents are spotlighted on first introduction. Give away your work as business and personal gifts and be generous with samples to potential clients, especially business or organizational ones.

Volunteer to provide your services where your products will get exposure in return for a mention in the program: Do the nametags for a garden club function, for instance, or make a clock for the coach's gift to be presented at a sports banquet. Whenever appropriate (and with the client's permission, of course) put your business name and phone number on your creations. If you do quality work, this may be the only advertising you need.

Quickly build a portfolio using actual samples of both the items you give away and any you are hired to do. For crafts that don't tuck neatly in a portfolio, photograph them. One technique for getting new business, as well as portfolio material, is to do makeovers. Keep an eye out for menus, doorknob hangers, magnets, and the like, that you feel you can improve. Tactfully show the "after" version to the original's owner and offer your services for the next anticipated update.

Craft shows are another venue where computer crafts can be marketed. The advantage to this is that you can sell products you have already made as well as take orders for custom products. Packaging and display are important factors at a craft show. Visit several shows to find out how veteran crafters present their work. Also be sure to check the rules for craft shows in which you intend to exhibit, to make sure that computer crafts are allowed.

Bridal shows, swap meets, and even home parties are other possible ways to get exposure for your products. Look around and you're sure to find marketing ideas as creative as the things you make.

BYE-BYE, MICKEY

When you begin to sell the products you make, the rules change as to what you can and can't use in the way of graphics. Read carefully the license agreements that came with your clip art packages or with other programs that include clip art. Some can be used on anything, others can be used with permission, and others you'll have to forget about.

You must also have rights to any items you scan. For instance, if a customer brings you a portrait with a studio signature on the front or a copyright notice on the back, you can't legally scan it without permission from the studio.

Licensed characters and sports team logos are the biggest no-no of all. It is rumored that if you try to scan Mickey

Mouse, your modem will automatically dial Disney headquarters and report you!

Anyone in this business should have a good working knowledge of copyright issues. As a side benefit, you'll also learn how to protect your own original work from copyright infringement.

BUSINESS RESOURCES

I've listed some good books and periodicals below for crafts businesses and for DTP businesses. You'll find a wealth of information in them, but keep in mind that a computer crafts business differs from a typical crafts business in that the investment in capital equipment is a significant factor. It differs from the typical desktop publishing business in that finished products are sold. (Because desktop publishers usually provide a master document to a client, their work is considered a service rather than a product.)

Crafting for Dollars: Turn Your Hobby into Serious Cash
Sylvia Landman
ISBN 0–7615–0442–7
Prima Publishing
http://www.primapublishing.com

Desktop Publishing: Dollars & Sense
Scott Anderson
ISBN 0–936085–51–7
Blue Heron Publishing

Desktop Publishing Success: How to Start and Run a Desktop Publishing Business
Felix Kramer and Maggie Lovaas
ISBN 1–55623–424–4
Irwin Professional Publishing

Handmade for Profit: Hundreds of Secrets to Success in Selling

Arts and Crafts
Barbara Brabec
ISBN 0–87131–812–1
M. Evans & Co.

Home Office Computing Magazine
(800) 288–7812
http://www.smalloffice.com

Price Guide for Desktop Services
Robert Brenner and Dawn Essman
ISBN 0–929535–15–4
Brenner Information Group
P.O. Box 721000
San Diego, CA 92172–1000
http://www.brennerbooks.com

Pricing Tables: Desktop Services
Robert Brenner
ISBN 0–929535–16–2
Brenner Information Group
P.O. Box 721000
San Diego, CA 92172–1000
http://www.brennerbooks.com

*Start and Run a Profitable
Craft Business: A Step by Step
Business Plan*
William G. Hynes
ISBN 1–55180–071–3
Self-Counsel Press Inc.

*Start Your Own Desktop
Publishing Business*
ISBN 0–13–603283–4
Prentice Hall Publishing

*To Market, To Market: How to
Start a Computer Crafts Business
and Make It Successful*
Darleen Araujo
teapotd@snowcrest.net
http://pages.prodigy.net/teapot.
    designs/teapot.htm

Where to Find It:
Listed by Item

Unfortunately, there's no such thing as a computer crafts store (yet!), so you might have to make a few stops before you have all the media and supplies you need. To make the shopping a little easier, here I've categorized all the items mentioned in this book and a few more things as well. Contact information for specific suppliers (such as Micro Format, Queblo, and so on) is located in Appendix C.

Printable Media

	Computer/Office Superstores	Mass Merchandisers	Micro Format	Craft Stores	DTP Catalogs	Paper Stores	Weber-Valentine	Art/Drafting Stores	Other
3M Post-It Signs and Notes	•	•			•				
adhesive-backed fabric				•					2
adhesive vinyl (clear)*			•						13
adhesive vinyl (white)*			•				•		13
appliqué film (clear matte and clear gloss)*					10			•	
appliqué film (white)*			•		•			•	
archival paper*	•		•						
artist's canvas *	•		•					•	
audiocassette inserts				•	9				
back print film*	3		•						
banner paper*	4								
brochure (preprinted)	•				•	•		•	
brochure (white, scored)*	3								
business card sheets	•	•	•		•	•		•	
business card sheets (glossy finish)			•	•					6
certificate/border paper	•	•	•	•	5	•			
clock faces (perforated)				•	•			•	6
card stock (coated)*	•		•	•	•	•		•	1
card stock (plain)	•	•	•	•	•	•	•	•	
coated paper*	•	•	•	•			•	•	
doorknob hangers					•				
double-coated paper (2 sides)*	•	•	•						
dual-coated paper (2 colors)*							•		

Item	Computer/Office Superstores	Mass Merchandisers	Micro Format	Craft Stores	DTP Catalogs	Paper Stores	Weber-Valentine	Art/Drafting Stores	Other
card stock, exotic (glossy, linen, etc.)						•			1
fabric carrier			•						
fabric sheets	•			•					
gift boxes (perforated)									1
gift tags (perforated)			•	•					
greeting card paper*	•								
greeting card paper (deckle edge)*								•	
greeting card paper (glossy)*	•		•						15
heat-activated color change paper		•	•						
heat transfer paper*	•	•	•	•			•		7
jigsaw puzzle blanks			•						8
label stock (full sheet)	•				•	•			
label stock (removable)	•	•			•	•			
labels (address and media)	•	•			•	•			
labels (clear)*	•	•			•	•			
letterhead (preprinted)	•	•	•		•	•			
metallic film			•					•	16
metallic paper*				•				•	
metallic paper (adhesive-backed)*								•	6
name tag kits	•				•	•			
newsletters (preprinted)					•				
note cards/invitations					•				
novelty recycled (blue jeans, grass, etc.)					12				
personal planner pages	•								

PRINTABLE MEDIA (CONTINUED)

	Computer/Office Superstores	Mass Merchandisers	Micro Format	Craft Stores	DTP Catalogs	Paper Stores	Weber-Valentine	Art/Drafting Stores	Other
photo film (glossy finish)*	•						•	•	15
photo paper (glossy finish)*		•	•				•	•	15
photo paper (semi-gloss finish)*							•		
photo paper (matte finish)*			•				•		15
photo stickers *	14		•						15
plain paper (white and colored)	•	•		•	•	•		•	
postcards (preprinted)	•				•				
printable presentation folders					•	•			
rotary card sheets	•				•				
satin-finish fabric*			•	•				•	
satin-finish fabric (adhesive-backed)									16
self-laminating cards	•				•				
shrink plastic sheets*	•	•	•	•					
table tents					•				
textured artist's paper*							•	•	

	Computer/Office Superstores	Mass Merchandisers	Micro Format	Craft Stores	DTP Catalogs	Paper Stores	Weber-Valentine	Art/Drafting Stores	Other
tickets					10				
translucent vellum*			•				•		
transparency film*	•	•	•		•	•	•	•	
Tyvek*							•		
velour paper				•					1,6
Virtual Reality 3D Paper			•						
visor stock (perforated)					9				
waterslide decal film (not for inkjets)									11
watercolor paper			•	•				•	
window cling film (clear)*			•	•				•	
window cling film (white)*			•					•	

NOTES:

*indicates inkjet coated
1. rubber stamp stores/suppliers
2. fabric and closeout stores
3. Canon dealers
4. Hewlett Packard dealers
5. especially Baudville, Idea Art
6. Eystad's Desktop Publishing Supplies
7. transfer supply companies
8. Compoz-a-Puzzle
9. Paper Direct
10. Queblo
11. Labco, Detail Master, hobby shops
12. LeDesktop
13. D. Brooker and Associates
14. Epson dealers
15. camera stores
16. Klassic Specialties

GENERAL CRAFT SUPPLIES

Find these in craft stores, mass merchandisers (who have a craft department), fabric stores (who have a craft department), and craft supply catalogs. Listed below are generic names of items; some are followed by a few of the brand names available:

acrylic coating spray:
    Patricia Nimock/Plaid, Krylon
batting
craft foam sheets: Darice Foamies
decorative-edge scissors:
    Fiskars, McGill
decoupage coating: Mod Podge,
    Liquid Laminate
dimensional paint: Tulip
double-sided adhesive sheets:
    ThermoWeb
embellishments (charms, buttons,
    doilies, wiggly eyes, pompoms,
    and so on)
fabric stiffener: Plaid
fabric transfer medium: Aleene's
    Transfer-It, Plaid Picture This
finished wooden plaque
fixative spray: Blair, Krylon
foam core posterboard: Bienfang
glitter glue: Crayola, Duncan
    Glitter Writers
glitter spray: Glitterama
hobby knife: X-Acto
hot glue gun and glue sticks
pin backs
spray glue: 3M
thick white glue: Aleene's Tacky Glue
watercolor paper

RUBBER STAMPING/ SCRAPBOOKING SUPPLIES

Find these in specialty stores, in craft stores, and through suppliers that cater to rubber stampers and scrapbookers.

circle cutters: Olfa, NT, Family
    Treasures

clear vinyl checkbook and business
    card holders
corner punches/rounders: McGill,
    Marvy Uchida
corner scissors: Fiskars
craft punches: Fiskars, McGill,
    Marvy Uchida
die-cut paper shapes
embossing powder
exotic papers and card stock
glue pen
metallic foil
mounting dots
narrow double-sided adhesive tape:
    Wonder Tape, Miracle Tape
scoring tool
tassels

SEWING SUPPLIES

Find these in a fabric store, fabric department, or in a sewing notions catalog.

barrette made for fabric covering
fusible (iron-on) adhesive:
    Heat-n-Bond
fusible webbing: Aleene's Fusible
    Web, Wonder Under
handheld rotary cutter and blades:
    Fiskars, Olfa
iron-on vinyl: HeatnBond
lace trim
perforating wheel: Fiskars, Olfa
ribbon

OFFICE SUPPLIES

Find these in office supply superstores, mass merchandisers (in the school or office supply department), and office supply catalogs.

announcement-size envelopes
booklet envelopes (6 x 9-inch)
clear cover: Con-Tact
clear vinyl (shipping) tape
colored staples
double-sided foam tape

foam core posterboard: Bienfang
guillotine paper trimmer: Boston
hook-and-loop fastener dots: Velcro
inkjet cleaning paper
personal paper trimmer: Fiskars
presentation portfolios
pressure-sensitive laminating sheets:
   C-Line
removable adhesive applicator: Dry
   Line, Tombo
removable adhesive glue stick: 3M
   Post-It
removable tape: 3M Post-It
   Correction & Cover Up Tape
rotary card sleeves: Rolodex
rotary trimmer (desktop): Boston,
   Fiskars
rubber cement
spray glue: 3M
three-ring binders
videocassette cases
wet-erase pen for overhead transparencies

LAMINATING SUPPLIES

A limited supply of laminators and
pouches is available at most office
superstores. For a larger selection and
specialty items such as folder lamination pouches, contact the lamination
supply sources (such as Cathy's
Creations and USI) listed in Appendix
C under Media/Materials Suppliers and
Services.

PLASTIC SNAP-TOGETHER PRODUCTS

Be on the lookout for snap-in products
in craft stores and mass merchandisers
in the kid's craft and counted cross-
stitch departments. Additionally, Micro
Format, photo supply houses, and
transfer supply catalogs carry a selection of these. The ProGold line of business card insert products is carried
exclusively at Office Depot.

TRANSFER BLANKS

A limited selection of items that accept
transfers can be found at craft stores
and mass merchandisers. Many more
items can be ordered from transfer supply companies. In particular, Hanes
Printables (1–800–HANES–2U) is an
excellent source for a wide variety of
transfer blanks in small quantities.

BUSINESS SERVICES

Most quick-print shops and office supply superstores offer laminating, comb
binding, perfect binding, and color
photocopying services. For heavy-duty
cutting, check with quick-print shops
or traditional printers. Kinko's, open
24 hours a day, is an especially good
source for these business services.

Kinko's store locator
   (800) 743–2679

Canon Color Copier locator
   (800) 652–2666

MISCELLANEOUS SUPPLIES

adhesive-backed magnetic sheets   For
sheets thin enough for easy cutting (15
mil or less), choose CraftMAGic sheets
(in craft stores and departments) or
PrintPaks Magnet Supplies Paks (available at craft stores, mass merchandisers, computer and office supply superstores, and Toys R Us); or order business card-size magnet sheets from The
Paper Path.

burnishing tools: X-Acto   Available at
art/drafting supply stores or office
superstores (drafting supplies department). The one I use is from X-Acto
and has a black plastic "spatula" on
one end and a metal ball-shaped tip on
the other end.

clear vinyl photo albums   Available
from Cathy's Creations.

confetti   Specialty confetti can be found in party stores, craft stores, rubber stamp stores, or by mail from Confetti Spaghetti.

Country Keeper by New Berlin Obtainable in cross-stitch departments or by mail from Mary Jane's Cross' N Stitch.

flocking (fuzzy stuff in small jars) Available from rubber stamp supply sources.

freezer paper: Reynolds   Available at grocery stores, well camouflaged beside the waxed paper and aluminum foil.

holographic film   May be ordered from D. Brooker and Associates.

laser-color foil: IbiFoil, LaserColor, ColorFX   Available in office supply superstores, usually near the binding supplies, or from most desktop publishing paper catalogs.

Liquid Appliqué (special paint pens; paint puffs when heated)   Available in craft stores and rubber stamp supply stores and sources.

padding compound   Available from paper stores or your local printer.

paper corrugator/crimper (or tube wringer)   Available in art departments with painting supplies or in rubber-stamping stores.

UV-resistant acrylic coating spray: Krylon #1305   Available at craft stores.

wood veneer tape   Available where woodworking supplies are sold.

Where to Find It: Listed by Vendor

HARDWARE MANUFACTURERS

Alps Electric, USA
3553 N. 1st St.
San Jose, CA 95134
(800) 825–2577
(408) 432–6000
(408) 432–6035 fax
http://www.alpsusa.com/
MicroDry printers and media

Apple Computer, Inc.
1 Infinite Loop
Cupertino, CA 95014
(800) 767–2775
(408) 996–1010
http://www.apple.com
inkjet printers and media

Canon CCSI
P.O. Box 2734
Costa Mesa, CA 92626
(800) 848–4123
http://www.usa.canon.com
inkjet printers and media

Compaq
(800) 888-0220
http://www.compaq.com
inkjet printers

Epson America, Inc.
20770 Madrona Ave.
Torrance, CA 90503
(800) 289–3776, ext. 3000
(310) 782–0770
(310) 782–5220 fax
http://www.epson.com/
inkjet printers and media

Hewlett Packard
16399 West Bernardo Dr.
San Diego, CA 92127–1899
(800) 752–0900
http://www.hp.com
inkjet printers and media

Lexmark
740 New Circle Rd. N.W.
Lexington, KY 40550
(800) 539–6275
http://www.lexmark.com
inkjet printers and media

Okidata
(800) 654-8326
http://www.okidata.com
inkjet printers

Play Incorporated
2890 Kilgore Rd.
Rancho Cordova, CA 95670
(916) 851–0800
(916) 631–0705 fax
http://www.play.com
Snappy video capture system

Xerox
800 Long Ridge Rd.
Stamford, CT 06904
(800) 275-9376
http://www.xerox.com
inkjet printers and media

SOFTWARE SUPPLIERS

Adobe Systems Incorporated
345 Park Ave.
San Jose, CA 95110–2704
(800) 833–6687
(408) 536–6000
(408) 537–6000 fax
http://www.adobe.com/
Adobe PhotoDeluxe

Apple Computer, Inc.
1 Infinite Loop
Cupertino, CA 95014
(800) 767–2775
(408) 996–1010
http://www.apple.com
Appleworks (formerly ClarisWorks)

Austin-James
P.O. Box 1126
Fort Wayne, IN 46856–1126
(800) 426–3728
htsmaker@aol.com
http://www.austin-james.com
Hanes T-ShirtMaker & More

Avery Dennison
50 Pointe Dr.
Brea, CA 92821
(800) 462–8379 (GO AVERY)
(800) 831–2496 fax
http://www.avery.com/
Printertainment kits, LabelPro,
MacLabelPro

Blue Squirrel
170 W. Election Dr., Ste. 125
Draper, UT 84020
(801) 523–1063
(801) 523–1064 fax
ClickBook
http://www.bluesquirrel.com

Broderbund Software, Inc.
(a division of The Learning
Company)
P.O. Box 6121
Novato, CA 94948
(800) 548–1798
(415) 382–4419 fax
webmaster@broder.com
http://www.broder.com
Print Shop Premier Edition,
ClickArt clip art series

CompUSA, Inc.
14951 N. Dallas Pkwy.
Dallas, TX 75240
(800) 266–7872
http://www.compusa.com
computer superstore chain

Computer City
300 W. 3rd St., Ste. 1500
Fort Worth, TX 76102
(800) 843–2489
http://www.computercity.com
computer superstore chain

Corel
1600 Carling Ave.
Ottawa, Ontario
Canada K1Z 8R7
(800) 772–6735
(613) 728–3733
(613) 761–9176 fax
http://www.corel.com/
Corel Print House, CorelDraw,
clip art

Deneba Software
7400 S.W. 87th Ave.
Miami, FL 33173
(305) 596–5644
(305) 273–9069 fax
deneba@aol.com
http://www.deneba.com/
Canvas (draw software)

DogByte Development
612 Moulton Ave., Ste. 7
Los Angeles, CA 90031
(800) 936–4298
(213) 221–9222
http://www.dogbyte.com
Stationery Store, Frame-It, Label
Store Design Solution, Sticker Store
Design Solution

HobbyWare
P.O. Box 501996
Indianapolis, IN 46250
(800) 768–6257
(972) 562–5411
(972) 562–9287 fax
http://www.hobbyware.com
Pattern Maker for Cross Stitch

IMSI
1895 Francisco Blvd. East
San Rafael, CA 94901–5506
(800) 833–8082
(415) 257–3000
(415) 257–3565 fax
http://www.imsisoft.com
clip art

Inclipz Graphic Inc.
P.O. Box 783
Pleasant Grove, UT 84062
(801) 785–3480
http://www.inclipz.com
clip art

Inspire Graphics
P.O. Box 935
Pleasant Grove, UT 84062
(801) 785–3878
(801) 796–8393 fax
http://www.inspiregraphics.com
Lettering Delights (novelty fonts),
clip art

Jasc Software, Inc.
P.O. Box 44997
Eden Prairie, MN 55344–2697
(800) 622–2793
(612) 930–9800
(612) 930–9172 fax
orders@jasc.com
http://www.jasc.com
Paint Shop Pro

The Learning Company
1 Athenaeum St.
Cambridge, MA 02142
(617) 494–1200
(617) 494–5700
(617) 494–1219 fax
http://www.learningco.com
See Broderbund Software, Inc.,
Mindscape, SoftKey International
Inc.

MetaCreations Corporation
6303 Carpinteria Ave.
Carpinteria, CA 93013
(805) 566–6200
(805) 566–6385 fax
hscsales@aol.com
http://www.metatools.com
Kai's SuperGoo (formerly Kai's
PowerGoo), Kai's Photo Soap

Micro Blvd.
928 N. Industrial Park Dr.
Orem, UT 84057
(800) 975–6300
(801) 229–9090
http://www.microblvd.com
Instant T-Shirt & Poster Deluxe

Micrografx
1303 E. Arapaho Rd.
Richardson, TX 75081
(888) 216–9281
(972) 234–1769
(972) 994–6475 fax
http://www.creatacard.com/
http://www.micrografx.com
American Greetings CreataCard,
Windows Draw 6 Print Studio

Microsoft Corp.
1 Microsoft Way
Redmond, WA 98052–6399
(800) 426–9400
(425) 882–8080
http://www.microsoft.com/
Greetings Workshop, Publisher 98

MicroWarehouse
1720 Oak St.
Lakewood, NJ 08701
(800) 397–8508
(732) 942–2502 fax
http://www.warehouse.com
computer software, hardware, and
supplies catalog

Mindscape (a division of The
Learning Company)
88 Rowland Wy.
Novato, CA 94945
(415) 895-2000
(415) 895-2102
http://www.mindscape.com
Printmaster Gold

MySoftware Company
2197 E. Bayshore Rd.
Palo Alto, CA 94303
(800) 325–3508
(650) 473–3620 fax
http://www.mysoftware.com
MyAdvanced LabelDesigner

New Vision Technologies Inc.
38 Auriga Dr., Unit 13
Nepean, Ontario
Canada K0G 1J0
(800) 387–0732
(613) 727–8184
(613) 727–8190 fax
info@tfclipart.com
http://www.nvtech.com
clip art

PC Connection/Mac Connection
528 Route 13
Attn: Sales
Milford, NH 03055
(800) 800–0018
http://www.macconnection.com
computer software, hardware, and
supplies catalog

Parsons Technology
P.O. Box 100
Hiawatha, IA 52233
(800) 973–5111
(319) 395–9626
http://www.parsonstech.com
Announcements Deluxe

PrintPaks
513 N.W. 13th Ave., Ste. 202
Portland, OR 97209
(800) 774–6860
(503) 295–6564
(800) 774–6851 fax
printpaks@aol.com
http://www.printpaks.com/
multimedia craft kits

Provo Craft
285 E. 900 S.
Provo, UT 84606
(801) 377–4311
(801) 373–1901 fax
clip art

Sierra On-Line, Inc.
3380 146th Place, SE
Bellevue, WA 98007
(800) 757–7707
(425) 649–9800
(402) 393–3224 fax
http://www.sierra.com
Print Artist

SoftKey International Inc.
(a division of The Learning
Company)
1 Athenaeum St.
Cambridge, MA 02142
(800) 227–5609
(617) 494–1200
(617) 494–1219 fax
http://www.learningco.com
Calendar Creator, clip art

Soul Sisters Designs
Attn: Maggie Martin
4750 N. Central Ave., #8D
Phoenix, AZ 85012
http://members.aol.com/palmaggie/
    amainpg01.htm
phxmaggie@aol.com
Print Artist add-ons

Specialty Publications
P.O. Box 1545
Florissant, MO 63031
easyway@inlink.com
http://www.iwc.com/easyway/
Print Artist add-ons

Stratus Direct
(800) 250–3988
http://www.stratusdirect.com
crafting clip art catalog

SNX (formerly Synex)
692 10th St.
Brooklyn, NY 11215
(800) 619–0299
(718) 499–6293
(718) 768–3997 fax
synex@snx.com
http://www.snx.com/envlfeat.html
MacEnvelope

3M
3M Center, Building 224–5N–38
St. Paul, MN 55144–1000
(800) 364–3577
http://www.mmm.com/
    notesandsigns/
Post-It Notes Design Software

MEDIA/MATERIALS SUPPLIERS AND SERVICES

Accu-Cut Systems, Inc.
1035 E. Dodge St.
Fremont, NE 68025
(800) 288–1670
(402) 721–4134
(402) 721–5778 fax
info@accucut.com
http://www.accucut.com/
die-cutting tools and supplies
catalog

Aleene's
85 Industrial Way
Buellton, CA 93427
(800) 825–3363
(805) 688–8638 fax
http://www.aleenes.com
craft supplies manufacturer

American Science & Surplus
3605 W. Howard St.
Skokie, IL 60076
(847) 982–0874
(800) 934–0722 fax
http://www.sciplus.com
miscellaneous supplies catalog

Artist's Club
P.O. Box 8930
Vancouver, WA 98668
(800) 845–6507
(360) 260–8877 fax
art supply catalog

Art Today
c/o ZEDCOR, INC.
3420 N. Dodge, Suite Z
Tucson, AZ 85716–5305
(520) 881–8101
e-mail@zedcor.com
http://www.arttoday.com
clip art subscription service

Avery Dennison
50 Pointe Dr.
Brea, CA 92821
(800) 462–8379 (GO AVERY)
(800) 831–2496 fax
http://www.avery.com/
labels, self-laminating cards, and
other media

Badge-A-Minit
345 N. Lewis Ave.
Oglesby, IL 61348
(800) 223–4103
(815) 883–9696 fax
http://www.badgeaminit.com
button-making equipment catalog

Baudville, Inc.
5380 52nd St. SE
Grand Rapids, MI 49506
(800) 728–0888
(616) 698–0888
(616) 698–0554 fax
funstuff@baudville.com
sales@baudville.com
http://www.baudville.com
desktop publishing paper catalog

D. Brooker and Associates
Rt. 1, Box 12A
Derby, IA 50068
(515) 533–2103
(515) 533–2104 fax
dbrooker@netins.net
http://www.netins.net/showcase/
  ever-stuff
Holo-Graf-Craft kits

Capi's Creations
6451 N. Kimball Ave.
Lincolnwood, IL 60645–3813
(847) 673–3572
(847) 673–9950 fax
capiii@prodigy.com
capiiii@aol.com
rubber stamping supplies

Chartpak
1 River Rd.
Leeds, MA 01053
(800) 628–1910
(800) 762–7918 fax
inkjet media manufacturer

Clotilde
2 Sew Smart Way
Louisiana, MO 63353–3000
(800) 772–2891
(573) 754–5511
(573) 754–3109 fax
http://www.clotilde.com/
sewing notions catalog

Compoz-a-Puzzle, Inc.
1 Robert Lane
Glen Head, NY 11545
(800) 343–5887
(516) 759–1102 fax
http://www.composapuzzle.com/
Puzzle Clonzz manufacturer

Confetti Spaghetti
P.O. Box 1526
Anaheim, CA 92803–1526
(714) 491–3565
specialty confetti (send $1.50 for a
"sprinkle" and catalog)

Craft King
P.O. Box 90637
Lakeland, FL 33804
(800) 769–9494
(941) 648–2969
(941) 648–2972 fax
craftkng@gate.net
http://www.auntie.com/cking/
art/craft supplies catalog

Crafty Accessories
918 Greencrest St.
Prattville, AL 36067
(334) 365–1844
(334) 365–3045 fax
sxpl96a@prodigy.net
http://pages.prodigy.net/cathymc/
  accessories.htm
laminating supplies

Creative Accents, Inc.
951 W. Rio Zuni
Green Valley, AZ 85614
(520) 648–0791
(520) 529–8734 fax
marolfe@aol.com
http://www.mho.net/t-tutor/
transfer supplies

CyberCraft
734 Merrimac Way
Brick, NJ 08724
(732) 785–2682
cybercraft@usa.net
computer crafting supplies

Detail Master
P.O. Box 1465
Sterling, VA 20167
(888) 338–5798
waterslide decal film

Dick Blick
P.O. Box 1267
695 Route 150
Galesburg, IL 61402
(800) 447–8192
(309) 343–6181
(800) 621–8293 fax
info@dickblick.com
http://www.dickblick.com/
art/craft supplies catalog

Discount School Supply
P.O. Box 7636
Spreckels, CA 93962
(800) 627–2829
(800) 879–3753 fax
http://www.earlychildhood.com
art/craft supplies catalog

Duncan
5673 E. Shields Ave.
Fresno, CA 93727
(800) 237–2642
(209) 291–4444 fax
http://www.duncan-enterprises.com
craft supplies manufacturer

Eystad's Desktop Publishing
Supplies
334 S. Broadway
Pitman, NJ 08071
(609) 256–2663
(609) 582–5138 fax
dqpl11a@prodigy.com
http://www.edps-nj.com
desktop publishing and computer
crafting supplies

Ellison Educational Equipment
25862 Commercentre Dr.
Lake Forest, CA 92630–8804
(800) 253–2238
(949) 598–8822
(800) 253–2240 fax
(949) 598–8840 fax
info@ellison.com
http://www.ellison.com
die-cutting tools and supplies
catalog

Expressive Impressions
1225 N. Dubonnet Ct.
Agoura, CA 91301
(818) 707–1225
(818) 706–1313 fax
envylady@earthlink.net
papercrafts supplies

Factory Direct Craft Supply
P.O. Box 16
315 Conover Dr.
Franklin, OH 45005
(800) 252–5223
(513) 743–5955
(800) 269–8741 fax
(513) 743–5500 fax
http://www.crafts2urdoor.com
art/craft supplies catalog

Family Treasures
14540 S.W. 136th St.
Miami, FL 33186–6762
(305) 252–2027
(305) 252–4023 fax
(800) 891–3520 fax
http://www.knowledgeware.com/itc/
scrapbooking supplies catalog

Fidelity
P.O. Box 155
Minneapolis, MN 55440–0155
(800) 326–7555
(800) 842–2725 fax
graphic products catalog

Fiskars
7811 W. Stuart Ave.
Wausau, WI 54401
(715) 842–2091
(715) 848–5528 fax
questions@fiskars.com
http://www.fiskars.com/
crafting tools manufacturer

Forever USA
60 N. Harrison Ave., Ste. 36
Congers, NY 10920
(800) 762–2679
(914) 267–3392
(914) 267–3398 fax
http://www.foreverusa.com
transfer supplies

Hanes Printables
P.O. Box 11126
Fort Wayne, IN 46856–1126
(800) 426–3728
http://www.hanes2u.com
transfer supplies

Idea Art
P.O. Box 291505
Nashville, TN 37229–1505
(800) 433–2278
(800) 435–2278 fax
http://www.ideaart.com
desktop publishing paper catalog

Jackson-Hirsh, Inc.
700 Anthony Trail
Northbrook, IL 60062
(800) 828–5053
(800) 344–5054 fax
lamination supplies catalog

Jacquard Products
Rupert, Gibbon & Spider
P.O. Box 425
Healdsburg, CA 95448
(800) 442-0455
(707) 433-9577
(707) 433-4906 fax
info@jacquardproducts.com
http://www.jacquardproducts.com
silk printing kits

Janlynn Cre8
34 Front St.
Indian Orchard, MA 01151
(800) 445–5565
(413) 543-7500
(413) 543-7505 fax
http://www.computercrafting.com
software, media and materials, kits

Joslin Photo Puzzle Co.
P.O. Box 914
Southampton, PA 18966
(215) 357-8346
(215) 357-0307 fax
http://www.jigsawpuzzle.com
puzzle blanks for heat transfer

Kinko's Copy Center
(800) 743–2679 for store locations

Klassic Specialties
P.O. Box 4014
Cerritos, CA 90703
(562) 865-2988
(562) 865-2988 fax
klassicspec@earthlink.net
http://home.earthlink.net/
~klassicspec

Labco
27563 Dover
Warren, MI 48093–4764
http://www.mich.com/~labco
waterslide/decal film

Le Desktop
7860 E. McClain Dr.
Scottsdale, AZ 85260
(800) 533-3758
http://www.ledesktop.com
desktop publishing paper catalog

Letraset
40 Eisenhower Dr.
Paramus, NJ 07652
(800) 342–0124
(201) 845–6100
http://www.letraset.com
color-foil, preprinted paper

Marcel Marketing
1337 Newport St.
Denver, CO 80220
(303) 393–8605
marcelmarketing@prodigy.com
transfer supplies

Mary Jane's Cross 'N Stitch
1948 Keim Ct.
Naperville, IL 60565
(630) 355–0071
(630) 355–0396 fax
http://www.maryjanes.com
counted cross-stitch supplies

Micro Format, Inc.
830–3 Seton Ct.
Wheeling, IL 60090
(800) 333–0549
(847) 520–4699
(847) 520–0197 fax
mformat@wwa.com
http://www.paper-paper.com
inkjet media and plastic craft
products

Nancy's Notions
P.O. Box 683
333 Beichl Ave.
Beaver Dam, WI 53916–0683
(800) 833–0690
(800) 387–0809 (TDD)
(800) 255–8119 fax
http://www.nancysnotions.com/
sewing notions catalog

Nasco
901 Janesville Ave.
P.O. Box 901
Fort Atkinson, WI 53538–0901
(800) 558–9595
(920) 563–2446
(920) 563–8296 fax
info@nascofa.com
http://www.nascofa.com
art/craft supplies catalog

Neil Enterprises, Inc.
450 East Bunker Ct.
Vernon Hills, IL 60061
(800) 621–5584
(847) 549–7627
(847) 549–0349 fax
http://www.neilenterprises.com
snap-in products manufacturer

Office Depot, Inc.
2200 Old Germantown Road
Delray Beach, FL 33445
(800) 685–8800
http://www.officedepot.com
office superstore chain

Office Max
http://www.officemax.com
office superstore chain

Oriental Trading Company
P.O. Box 3407
Omaha, NE 68103–0407
(800) 228–2269
(402) 331–6800
(800) 327–8904 fax
http://www.oriental.com
miscellaneous supplies

Paper Direct, Inc.
100 Plaza Dr., 2nd Flr.
Secaucus, NJ 07094
(800) 443–2973
(201) 271–9601 fax
http://www.paperdirect.com
desktop publishing paper and
presentation supplies catalog

The Paper Path
3968 Frandon Ct.
Simi Valley, CA 93063
(805) 527–1402
(805) 527–1402 fax
lindamccann@prodigy.net
adhesive-backed business card
magnets

Paper Plus
(888) 727–3775 store locator
paper stores

Pearl Arts and Crafts
306 Canal St.
New York, NY 10013
(800) 451–7327
(212) 431–7932
(212) 431–5420 fax
http://www.pearlpaint.com
art/craft supplies stores and catalog

Plaid Enterprises
P.O. Box 2835
Norcross, GA 30091
(800) 842–4197
http://www.plaidonline.com
craft supplies manufacturer

Porter's Camera Store, Inc.
P.O. Box 628
Cedar Falls, IA 50613
(800) 553–2001
(800) 221–5329 fax
http://www.porters.com
photography supplies

Projects & More
1000 E. 14th St., Dept. 244
Plano, TX 75074–2903
(972) 424–8448
(972) 424–8448 fax
projects@juno.com
http://members.aol.com/projects4/
    homepage/homepage.htm
rubber stamping supplies

P.S. Ink
P.O. Box 705
Northfield, NJ 08225
(609) 641–5235
(609) 641–5235 fax
psinkmastr@aol.com
http://www.psinkmaster.com
inkjet media

QLT Imprint Supplies
95 Morton St.
New York, NY 10014
(800) 221–9832
(212) 691–1515
(212) 645–2734 fax
http://www.qlt.com
transfer supplies

Queblo
P.O. Box 8465
Mankato, MN 56002
(800) 523–9080
(800) 842–3371 fax
desktop publishing paper catalog

Quill
P.O. Box 94080
Palatine, IL 60094–4080
(800) 789–1331
(800) 789–8955 fax
http://www.quillcorp.com
office supplies and desktop publishing paper catalog

Rayven Inc.
431 Griggs St. N.
St. Paul, MN 55104
(800) 878–3776 (call for free
    samples)
(612) 642–1112
(612) 642–9497 fax
http://www.rayven.com
inkjet media manufacturer

Repeat-O-Type
665 State Hwy. 23
Wayne, NJ 07470-6892
(800) 288-3330
(973) 696-3330
(973) 694-7287 fax
http://www.repeatotype.com
inkjet ink (including pigmented)
and media

S&S Worldwide
P.O. Box 513
Colchester, CT 06415
(800) 243-9232
(860) 537-3451
(800) 566-6678 fax
(860) 537-2866 fax
service@snswwide.com
http://www.snswwide.com
art/craft supplies catalog

Sailor
121 Bethea Rd. #307
Fayetteville, GA 30214
(800) 248-4583
(770) 461-9081
(770) 461-8452 fax
glue pen manufacturer

Sawgrass Systems, Inc.
2233 Highway 17 N.
Mt. Pleasant, SC 29464
(803) 884-1575
http://www.sawgrassinc.com
inkjet transfer ink manufacturer

Seattle FilmWorks
P.O. Box 34725
Seattle, WA 98124
(800) 345-9675
(206) 281–1390
(206) 284-5337 fax
info@filmworks.com
http://www.filmworks.com
digital photo processing service

Stamp Cabana
5428 Touchstone Drive
Orlando, FL 32819
(407) 363–5530
http://www.stampcabana.com
rubber stamping supplies

Staples, Inc.
One Research Drive
Westborough, MA 01581
(508) 370–8500
http://www.staples.com
office superstores and catalog

3M
3M Center, Building 224–5N–38
St. Paul, MN 55144–1000
(800) 364–3577
http://www.mmm.com/
    notesandsigns/
Post-It Notes for inkjet and laser
printers

Tombo
4467–C Park Dr.
Norcross, GA 30093
(800) 835–3232
(770) 381–6800
(770) 381–9999 fax
adhesive applicator manufacturer

Transfer Technologies
RR1, Box 827
Thornton, NH 03223
(800) 639–3111
(603) 726–3800
(603) 726–3870 fax
info@brncorp.com
http://www.brncorp.com
transfer supplies

True Basic Inc.
12 Commerce Ave.
West Lebanon, NH 03784–1669
(800) 436–2111
(603) 298–7015 fax
sales@truebasic.com
http://www.truebasic.com/
    labels.html
labels

USI, Inc.
98 Fort Path Rd.
Madison, CT 06443–2264
(800) 243–4565
(203) 245–7337 fax
http://www.usi-laminate.com/
    HOME.tmpl
laminating supplies catalog

Viking Office Products
950 W. 190th
Torrance, CA 90502
(800) 711–4242
(800) 762–7329 fax
http://www.vikingop.com
office supplies and desktop publishing paper catalog

Visual Horizons
180 Metro Park
Rochester, NY 14623–2666
(800) 424–1011
(800) 424–5411 fax
http://www.storesmart.com
presentation supplies catalog

Wacky Wagon's Ladybug
16857 Miller Lane
Lawson, MO 64062
(816) 580–3434
(816) 296–3060 fax
wackey@primenet.com
http://www.wackywagon.com

Weber-Valentine
1099 E. Morse Ave.
Elk Grove Village, IL 60007
(800) 323–9642
(847) 439–7111
(847) 439–6887 fax
john@weber-valentine.com
http://www.weber-valentine.com
inkjet media

xpedx (formerly ResourceNet)
50 E. Rivercenter Blvd. #700
Covington, KY 41011
(606) 655–2000
(606) 655–8983 fax
http://www.xpedx.com
paper stores

Xyron
14698 North 78th Way
Scottsdale, AZ 85260
(800) 793–3523
(602) 443–9419
(602) 443–0118 fax
http://www.xyron.com
tape laminating systems

For More Information

MAGAZINES

Craft Creations
Ingersoll House, Delamare Rd.
Cheshunt, Hertfordshire
EN8 9ND United Kingdom
44 (0)181 885 2655
44 (0)181 808 0746 fax
craftcreations1@dial.pipex.com
http://www.craftcreations.com/

Creating Keepsakes
P.O. Box 2119
Orem, UT 84059
(888) 247–5282
(801) 225–2878 fax
http://www.creatingkeepsakes.com

Dynamic Graphics
6000 N. Forest Park Dr.
Peoria, IL 61614–3592
(800) 255–8800
dyngraphic@aol.com
http://www.dgusa.com

FamilyPC
P.O. Box 37008
Boone, IA 50037–0088
(800) 413–9749
familypc@aol.com
http://www.zdnet.com/familypc/

Flash Magazine
Riddle Pond Rd.
West Topsham, VT 05086
(800) 252–2599
(802) 439–6462
(802) 439–6463 fax
info@flashmag.com
http://www.flashweb.com

Rubber Stamper
P.O. Box 420
Manalapan, NJ 07726
(800) 969–7176
http://www.rubberstamper.com

BOOKS

*The Art of Rubber Stamping,
2nd edition*
Michelle Abel
ISBN 0–96–30756–2–4
Creative Press

*Blueprints on Fabric: Innovative
Uses for Cyanotype*
Barbara Hewitt
ISBN 0–934026–91–2
Interweave Press
http://www.interweave.com

Book on Demand Publishing
Rupert Evans
ISBN 1–881676–02–1
BlackLightning Publishing
(800) 252–2599
http://www.flashweb.com

*Click! 101 Computer Activities
and Art Projects for Kids and
Grown-Ups*
Lynn Bundeson, Kristin Marks,
and Hannah Hoël
ISBN 0–684–83215–1
Simon & Shuster
http://www.simonsays.com

Clip Art Crazy
Chuck Green
ISBN 0–201–88361–9
Peachpit Press
(800) 283–9444
http://www.peachpit.com

The Computer T-Shirt Book
Bernie Klopp and Linda Klopp
ISBN 0–9646444–0–1
Brainstorm Communications
(410) 668–4243

The Crafter's Guide to Glues
Tammy Young
ISBN 0–8019–8611–7
Chilton Book Company

The Crafts Supply Source Book: A Comprehensive Shop-by-Mail Guide for Thousands of Craft Materials, 4th edition
Margaret A. Boyd
ISBN 1–55870–441–8
Betterway Publications
(800) 289–0963

Cut It Out (and various other titles) Hot Off the Press
http://www.hotp.com

The Desktop Publishers Idea Book, Second Edition
Chuck Green
ISBN 0–679–78006–8
Random House Reference and Information Publishing
http://www.ideabook.com

Digital Camera Companion
Ben Sawyer and Ron Pronk
ISBN 1–57610–097–9
Coriolis Group Books
(800) 410–0192
(602) 483–0192
http://www.coriolis.com

The Envelope Mill
Haila Harvey
ISBN 1–56530–149–8
Summit Publishing Group

Fabric Photos
Marjorie Croner
ISBN 0–934026–53–X
Interweave Press
http://www.interweave.com

The Family PC Guide to Cool PC Projects
Sam Mead
ISBN 0–7868–8207–7
Hyperion Books

A Few Scanning Tips
Wayne Fulton
(972) 379–5692 fax
fulton@scantips.com
http://www.scantips.com

The Graphic Designer's Source Book
Poppy Evans
ISBN 0–89134–642–2
North Light Books
(800) 289–0963

Imagery on Fabric, 2nd edition
Jean Ray Laury
ISBN 1–57120–034–7
C & T Publishing
(800) 284–1114
http://www.ctpub.com

Kid's Computer Creations: Using Your Computer for Art & Craft Fun
Carol Sabbeth
ISBN 0–913589–92–6
Williamson Publishing
(800) 234–8791

The Needlecrafter's Computer Companion
Judy Heim
No Starch Press
ISBN 1–886411–01–8
http://www.nostarch.com

The Non-Designers Design Book
Robin Williams
ISBN 1–56609–159–4
Peachpit Press
(800) 283–9444
http://www.peachpit.com

PolyShrink Jewelry Techniques Book/Kit
Kit Zimmerman and Jo Rebeka
ISBN 0–9650993–0–X
Lucky Squirrel Press
(800) 462–4912
squirrel@rt66.com

The Quilter's Computer Companion
Judy Heim and Gloria Hansen
ISBN 1–886411–15–8
No Starch Press
http://www.nostarch.com

Recipes for Art and Craft Materials
Helen Roney Sattler
ISBN: 0–688131–99–9
Beech Tree Books

Roger C. Parker's One-Minute Designer
Roger C. Parker
ISBN 1–55828–593–8
MIS:Press
http://www.mispress.com

The T-Shirt Tutor (Book/Kit)
Mary Ann Rolfe
Creative Accents, Inc.
(520) 648–0791
marolfe@aol.com
http://www.mho.net/t-tutor/

VIDEOS

*The Easy Way to Print Artist,
Vols. 1 and 2*
Specialty Publications
P.O. Box 1545
Florissant, MO 63031
easyway@inlink.com
http://www.iwc.com/easyway/

WORLD WIDE WEB SITES

Although only a few sites are dedicated specifically to creative color printing, the World Wide Web abounds with ideas you can apply to your projects. You'll also find plenty of shareware and project templates to download. Many Web sites now include message boards and chat rooms so you get input from a variety of other consumers in addition to information posted by the Web site's owner.

Web addresses, or URLs (for Uniform Resource Locators), tend to change frequently, and it's no fun to type them in anyway. To get around this problem, we'll post an up-to-date, comprehensive list of links at:

The Color Printer Idea Book site
http://www.nostarch.com/cpib

In the meantime, here are a few of the more notable computer craft sites to whet your appetite:

Computer Crafts/Print Artist
Listserv Home Page
http://pages.prodigy.com/PAFUN/

CraftNet Village Computer Crafts
Message Board
http://www.craftnetvillage.com/
    message_board/computer_
    crafts/index.html

CreataCard Friends
http://members.tripod.com/
    ~cacfriends/

Creativity Online
http://www.parsonstech.com/
    creativestudio/index.html

Excite Computer Crafts Message
Board
http:// boards.excite.com
(Select Life & Style, then "Arts and Crafts" and look for the Computer Crafts/PALs folder.)

Graphic Greetings
http://www.wwvisions.com/craftbb/
    graphicgreetings.html

PALs@Home
http://www.snowcrest.net/
    mrogers/pals

Print Artist Home Page
http://www.printartist.com

PrintMaster Home Page
http://www.printmaster.com

Print Shop Home Page
http://www.printshop.com

Stratus Direct Computer
Scrapbooking
http://www.stratusdirect.com

T-Talk
http://www.hanes2u.com

ONLINE SERVICES

Every online service seems to be in a state of flux as emphasis shifts heavily to the Internet. The navigation information below could well be out of date by the time you read this. If so, check with your online service's directory, searching for the terms *computer crafts* or *print artist*. You may also want to search for areas relevant to the particular software you use.

America Online

Computer Crafts Discussion

Use keyword "crafts," choose the "Other Crafts" message board, and scroll down to the "Computer Crafts" folder.

Print Artist Resource Center

Use keyword "print artist," choose "Message Boards," and scroll down to a topic that interests you. With the same keyword, you can also find downloadable Print Artist templates under "Print Artist Projects."

CompuServe

There's not much computer crafting conversation going on at CompuServe, but there is a very active rubber stamping area with a lot to offer. The friendly frequenters of CompuServe's extensive crafting areas are known as "CISters." Use the GO word "HANDCRAFTS," which will take you to rubber stamp messages in Section 9, paper crafts in Section 7, and other handcrafts (including computer crafts) in Section 12.

Delphi

Go to the member communities index and do a search for either "graphics" or "Print Artist" to find the Graphics Printing/PA forum (232). From the Web, Delphi members can go to **http://www.delphi.com/mc/** to perform the search. Print Artist templates are also available through the forum.

Prodigy

Prodigy has long been the computer crafting hot spot online because of its large concentration of Print Artist enthusiasts, known as PALs (for Print Artist Lovers). On Prodigy Classic use the jump word "CraftsBB" and select "Crafts 1BB." Select "Computer Crafts" from the list of choices to reach the message area and download library.

Prodigy Internet has recently opened its computer craft message board in conjunction with Excite, so you don't have to be a Prodigy member to participate. See the Excite Computer Crafts Message Board listed under Web sites above to find it.

MAILING LISTS

All you need is an e-mail account and you can read the banter between computer craft enthusiasts, post your questions, and share computer craft ideas. Here are some lists you might want to consider subscribing to:

Computer Crafts/Print Artist Home page:
http://pages.prodigy.com/PAFUN/
To subscribe: send an e-mail message to **majordomo@listserv.prodigy. com** with **subscribe pafun [your e-mail address]** in the body of your message.

CreataCard Friends
Home page:
http://members.tripod.com/
~cacfriends/
To subscribe: Fill out the form at
http://www.onelist.com/subscribe.cgi/
cacfriends.

Epson-Inkjet
Home page:
http://www.leben.com/lists/
epson-inkjet
To subscribe: Send an e-mail message to **majordomo@leben.com**
with **subscribe epson-inkjet [your**
e-mail address] in the body of your
message.

PALs@Home
Home page:
http://www.snowcrest.net/
mrogers/pals
To subscribe: send an e-mail message to **listserv@home.ease.lsoft.com**
with **SUB PALS [your first and last**
name] in the body of the message.

KEY:

(m) *indicates info in manual or sales material*
(t) *indicates testing or exploration needed*

MANUFACTURER (OEM) ___*EPSON*___ (m)
MODEL NUMBER ___*STYLUS PRO XL*___ (m)

OEM CARTRIDGE PART NUMBERS: (m)
black ___*S020034*___
color(s) ___*S020036*___
specialty ___*SAWGRASS SUBLI-JET*___

BLACK INK IS:
❏ pigment based (t) (slow drying, waterproof)
☑ dye-based

ADJUSTMENT FOR BANNER PRINTING: ☑ not supported

_____
_____
_____

MAX. WEIGHT PAPER RECOMMENDED: (m)

_____

ADJUSTMENT FOR THICK PAPER (m): ❏ none
PRESS PAUSE THEN ALT + FONT
FLIP SWITCH IN FRONT OF CARTRIDGES

DRIVER VERSION INSTALLED: (t) *POWER PRINT 3.0.2*

TO REVERSE IMAGE (m or t):
❏ backprint film or transfer paper media option
☑ flip horizontal command in print settings
❏ perform in application before printing

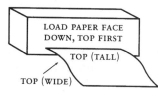

☑ front loading

LOAD PAPER FACE
DOWN, TOP FIRST
TOP (TALL)
TOP (WIDE)

❏ top or back loading

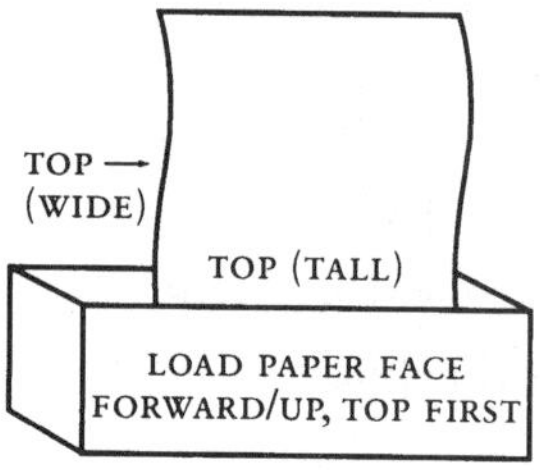

TOP →
(WIDE)
TOP (TALL)
LOAD PAPER FACE
FORWARD/UP, TOP FIRST

WIDE OR LANDSCAPE ORIENTATION

MARGINS:
top: (m) ___.12___
bottom: (m) ___.12___
left: (m) ___.12___
right: (m) ___.55___
to center: (t) _____

MAXIMUM DPI	COLOR	BLACK
PLAIN PAPER	720	720
PREMIUM PAPER	720	720

(m) — rows labeled on left

PRINT QUALITY ▶ MEDIA TYPE ▼	SUPER (720 dpi)	BEST (360 dpi)	DRAFT (180 dpi)	
PLAIN	✓	✓	✓	
Coated 360		✓		
Coated 720	✓	✓		
Transparency		✓		
HQ Glossy	✓			

TALL OR PORTRAIT ORIENTATION

LETTER : 8.26 × 10.33

MARGINS:
top: (m) ___.12___
bottom: (m) ___.55___
left: (m) ___.12___
right: (m) ___.12___
to center: (t) _____

KEY:

(m) *indicates info in manual or sales material*
(t) *indicates testing or exploration needed*

MANUFACTURER (OEM) _____ (m)
MODEL NUMBER _____ (m)

OEM CARTRIDGE PART NUMBERS: (m)
black _____
color(s) _____
specialty _____

BLACK INK IS:
❏ pigment based (t) (slow drying, waterproof)
❏ dye-based

ADJUSTMENT FOR BANNER PRINTING: ❏ not supported

_____
_____

MAX. WEIGHT PAPER RECOMMENDED: (m)

_____

ADJUSTMENT FOR THICK PAPER (m): ❏ none

_____
_____

DRIVER VERSION INSTALLED: (t)_____

TO REVERSE IMAGE (m or t):
❏ backprint film or transfer paper media option
❏ flip horizontal command in print settings
❏ perform in application before printing

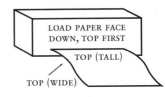

❏ front loading

LOAD PAPER FACE DOWN, TOP FIRST
TOP (TALL)
TOP (WIDE)

❏ top or back loading

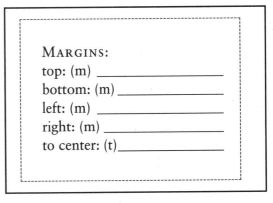

TOP → (WIDE)
TOP (TALL)
LOAD PAPER FACE FORWARD/UP, TOP FIRST

WIDE OR LANDSCAPE ORIENTATION

MARGINS:
top: (m) _____
bottom: (m) _____
left: (m) _____
right: (m) _____
to center: (t)_____

TALL OR PORTRAIT ORIENTATION

MARGINS:
top: (m) _____
bottom: (m) _____
left: (m) _____
right: (m) _____
to center: (t)_____

(m)	MAXIMUM DPI	COLOR	BLACK
	PLAIN PAPER		
(m)	PREMIUM PAPER		

PRINT QUALITY ▶				
MEDIA TYPE ▼				

W

X

THE NEEDLECRAFTER'S COMPUTER COMPANION

Hundreds of Easy Ways to Use Your Computer for Sewing, Quilting, Cross-Stitch, Knitting & More!

by JUDY HEIM

"This is the 'How-do-I-get-started-and-why?' book you've been waiting for. Don't hesitate." — THREADS MAGAZINE

Use your computer to create dazzling needlework designs as innovative as your imagination, or as traditional as the ones in Grandma's hope chest. You'll find opinionated reviews of quilting, cross-stitch, sewing, weaving, and knitting software; how to use your computer to convert family photos into cross-stitch patterns; how to download free craft patterns and get advice from needlework magazines online; where to find craft resources on the Internet and commercial online services (like CompuServe and America Online); how to use computers in your needlecraft business; and much more.

JUDY HEIM, a *PC World* magazine contributing editor, has been an avid sewer for over 30 years. She is also co-author of *The Quilter's Computer Companion*, and author of *I Lost My Baby, My Pickup, and My Guitar on the Information Highway* and *Internet for Cats*, all from No Starch Press.

> 460 pp., $34.95
> Includes two 3.5", high density, IBM-PC disks with trial versions of needlecraft software. Macintosh disk $0.75 additional.
> ISBN 1-886411-01-8

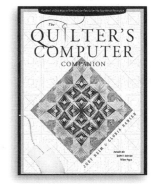

THE QUILTER'S COMPUTER COMPANION

Hundreds of Easy Ways to Turn the Cyber Revolution into Your Artistic Revolution

by JUDY HEIM *and* GLORIA HANSEN

This bestselling book shows you how to use your computer to design quilts and the best and cheapest way to do so. And you don't need the latest $4,000 Beyond-Pentium to do it. Design quilt blocks, templates, applique patterns, and stencils; print photos on muslin, organize your fabric stash, and prowl the Internet for art to use in your quilt designs; exchange e-mail with other quilters around the globe; and even put your quilts on display in cyberspace for everyone to see. Authors Judy Heim and Gloria Hansen show you, through hundreds of illustrations and step-by-step instructions, how to use the most popular drawing, painting, and quilt design software to achieve your own artistic vision.

JUDY HEIM, *PC World* magazine columnist and contributing editor, has been an avid sewer for over 30 years. She is the author of three other No Starch Press titles: *The Needlecrafter's Computer Companion, Internet for Cats,* and *I Lost My Baby, My Pickup, and My Guitar on the Information Highway.* She lives in Madison, Wisconsin.

GLORIA HANSEN has been quilting since 1982, and her innovative quilts have won many significant awards throughout the country. Gloria has appeared on cable television (even an MTV ad) and has self-published two successful quilt patterns; she is a frequent contributor to quilting publications, including *Art/Quilt Magazine* and *McCalls Quilting* and her unique fabrics have been featured in *Ladies Circle Patchwork Quilts* and *Miniworks* magazine. Gloria also contributed to the first edition of Judy Heim's *The Needlecrafter's Computer Companion*. She lives in central New Jersey.

352 pp., $29.95
Includes 16 full-color pages and hundreds of illustrations.
ISBN 1-886411-15-8

JUNO

Free E-Mail and More

by BOB RANKIN

Bob Rankin, recognized e-mail and Internet expert, shows you how to use Juno—the completely free, advertiser-supported Internet e-mail service—to do more than just send messages. You'll learn e-mail basics like how to Send, Receive, Reply, Forward, and Delete messages, as well as how to work with and manage folders. You'll learn the finer points of Netiquette, Spam, and e-mail privacy, and discover how to use simple e-mail commands with Juno to access almost anything on the Internet, including the World Wide Web, FTP libraries, Usenet newsgroups, and search engines. You'll also pick up some e-mail tricks, such as how to get stock market data, news, weather, and sports information; how to play games by e-mail; how to send free faxes; and much more!

BOB "DR. BOB" RANKIN is also the author of *The No B.S. Guide to Linux* and *Dr. Bob's Painless Guide to the Internet* (both from No Starch Press). He is well known for his "Accessing The Internet By E-mail" FAQ (read by hundreds of thousands of people around the world and translated into more than fifteen languages) and is the publisher of the *Internet TourBus* e-zine, an e-mail "tour" of fun and interesting things on the Net.

200 pp., $14.95
ISBN 1-886411-23-9

DR. BOB'S PAINLESS GUIDE TO THE INTERNET

& Amazing Things You Can Do with E-Mail

by BOB "DR. BOB" RANKIN

". . . simple, hassle-free net surfing with a minimum of reading . . ."
— NETGUIDE MAGAZINE

Whether you connect to the Internet through e-mail alone or the latest Netscape beta, *Dr. Bob's Painless Guide to the Internet* will show you how to use every Internet tool—not just the Web. You'll learn how to send and receive e-mail, find the cool and useful Web sites, search for and download the files you want, read newsgroups and subscribe to mailing lists, chat online, and more. Includes a glossary of terms and the "Internet Mini-Yellow Pages," with lots of useful Internet resources for you to enjoy right away.

BOB "DR. BOB" RANKIN *(see bio above)*

152 pp., $12.95
ISBN 1-886411-09-3

INTERNET FAMILY FUN

The Parent's Guide to Safe Surfing

by BONNIE BRUNO *with* JOEL COMM

Whether your family just got its first computer or you're a bunch of Internet veterans, *Internet Family Fun* will take you to the best and safest Web sites for your family fast—without a bunch of technical mumbo jumbo. With nearly 250 reviews of fun and informative sites, pre-screened for age appropriateness and family-friendly content, there's something for everyone from preschoolers to parents. Learn how to install and use filtering software; use the Internet for research; find hundreds of games and coloring pages for children; learn about our world through the use of online text, graphics, sound, and video; observe classrooms using the Internet; meet and correspond with families around the world; create your very own home page and more! And, learn how to keep your kids safe online while you're at it.

BONNIE BRUNO is the author of *The Young Reader's Bible* (Standard Publishing, co-authored with Carol Reinsma), *Close to Home* (Chariot Books), and *Mourning: The Prelude to Laughter* (Zondervan Publishers, 1994 Final Nominee for the Gold Medallion Award). She lives in Albany, Oregon.

JOEL COMM is president and CEO of InfoMedia, Inc., a Texas-based Internet content provider. He lives in Plano, Texas.

152 pp., $14.95
ISBN 1-886411-19-0

WRITER'S INTERNET SOURCEBOOK

Reviews of hundreds of websites especially for novelists, short story writers, journalists, poets, nonfiction authors, academics, playwrights, and business writers.

by MICHAEL LEVIN

The Internet offers extraordinary opportunities for writers for researching, marketing, and selling their work. The *Writer's Internet Sourcebook* reviews hundreds of websites of interest to writers. find out how to use the Internet to save hundreds of hours of library time; where to find online writing classes, support groups, newsgroups, and mailing lists for writers of fiction, nonfiction, drama, journalism, poetry and academic writing; descriptions and reviews of online magazines (zines); and how to use the Internet to find readers, subscribers, buyers, and online bookstores that can sell your work.

MICHAEL LEVIN, a popular novelist and non-fiction author, is heavily involved in the teaching and business of writing: He teaches in both the UCLA and NYU Writing Programs and he is on the board of the Author's Guild. His novels have been favorably reviewed in the *New York Times Book Review,* the *Los Angeles Times,* and the *Boston Herald.* He lives in the Los Angeles area.

256 pages, $16.95
ISBN 1-886411-11-5

THE GARDENER'S COMPUTER COMPANION

Hundreds of Easy Ways to Use Your Computer for Gardening

by BOB BOUFFORD

The Gardener's Computer Companion has all the information you need to use your computer for gardening, including a complete collection of software (over 60 programs to try!) to get you started. Save time and make your gardening more pleasurable by learning how to select gardening software and hardware, plan and manage your garden using your computer, and communicate with gardeners around the world.

295 pages, $39.95, CD-ROM
ISBN: 1-886411-18-2